WORDPERFECT 5.0/5.1

EASY REFERENCE GUIDE

JANET GIGLIA

Berkeley College
White Plains Campus

WM07AA
PUBLISHED BY
SOUTH-WESTERN PUBLISHING CO.
CINCINNATI, OH   DALLAS, TX   LIVERMORE, CA

ISBN: 0–538–61399–8

Library of Congress Catalog Card Number: 90–63286

1 2 3 4 5 6 7 8 9 H 9 8 7 6 5 4 3 2 1

Printed in the United States of America

Acquisitions Editor: Janie F. Schwark
Developmental Editor: Dianne S. Rankin
Production Editor: Carolyn Morgan
Designer: Nicola M. Jones
Marketing Manager: Al S. Roane

WordPerfect® is a registered trademark of WordPerfect Corporation.

PREFACE

WordPerfect®[1] 5.0/5.1 Easy Reference Guide is designed to help you access WordPerfect® commands quickly without having to use a large, complicated manual. A simple listing of the cursor key commands, command keys, and merge codes is provided at the beginning of the text along with easy-to-follow steps on how to format a disk and how to start WordPerfect. The functions are listed alphabetically for easy reference, and a detailed index is provided at the back of the book.

In many cases, the commands for WordPerfect version 5.0 and version 5.1 are the same. These commands are shown in dark blue type on a white background just as this preface is.

Where WordPerfect 5.0 and 5.1 keystroke commands differ, the 5.1 commands are shown on a light blue background as illustrated in this paragraph.
*   *Mouse commands are for version 5.1 only and appear in italics on a light blue background within or below the keystroke commands.*

A sample reference entry is shown on the following page.

Relax and enjoy using your *WordPerfect 5.0/5.1 Easy Reference Guide*!

Many thanks to my students, the staff, and administration at Berkeley College for their support. Special thanks to my husband, Bob, for all his understanding and encouragement.

Janet Giglia

[1]*WordPerfect is a registered trademark of WordPerfect Corporation.*

Sample Reference Entry

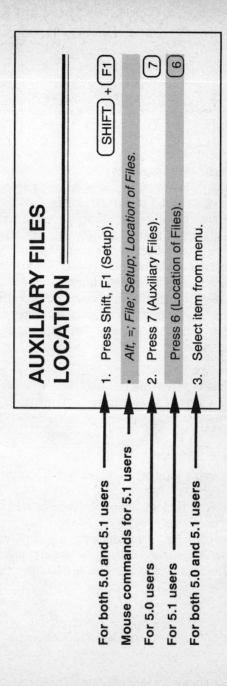

AUXILIARY FILES LOCATION

1. Press Shift, F1 (Setup).   SHIFT + F1

   • *Alt, =; File; Setup; Location of Files.*

2. Press 7 (Auxiliary Files).   7

   Press 6 (Location of Files).   6

3. Select item from menu.

For both 5.0 and 5.1 users

Mouse commands for 5.1 users

For 5.0 users

For 5.1 users

For both 5.0 and 5.1 users

iv

CURSOR COMMANDS

One character right   `→`

One character left   `←`

One line up   `↑`

One line down   `↓`

One word right   `CTRL` + `→`

One word left   `CTRL` + `←`

Advance a specific number of lines   `ESC` , `↑`

Delete a specific number of lines   `ESC` ,

                                            `CTRL` + `END`

Right end of line   `HOME` + `→`

Left end of line   `HOME` + `←`

Top of screen   `HOME` + `↑`

                                            or `-`

Bottom of screen   `HOME` + `↓`

                                            or `+`

Beginning of file before all codes   `HOME` ,

                                            `HOME` ,

                                            `HOME` , `↑`

Top of current page   `CTRL` + `HOME` ,

                                            `↑`

Bottom of current page   `CTRL` + `HOME` ,

                                            `↓`

GOTO a specific page	CTRL + HOME
	INPUT page no.
Previous page	PAGE UP *or* 9 PgUp
Top of next page	PAGE DOWN *or* 3 PgDn
Top of document	HOME , HOME , ↑
End of document	HOME , HOME , ↓
One column right	CTRL + HOME , →
One column left	CTRL + HOME , ←

COMMAND KEYS

Block	`ALT` + `F4`
	or `F12`
Bold	`F6`
Cancel	`F1`
Center	`SHIFT` + `F6`
Copy	`CTRL` + `F4`
Date/Outline	`SHIFT` + `F5`
Delete to End of Line	`CTRL` + `1 END`
Delete to End of Page	`CTRL` + `3 PgDn`
Delete Word	`CTRL` + `BKSP`
Enter	`ENTER`
Exit	`F7`
Flush Right	`ALT` + `F6`
Font	`CTRL` + `F8`
Footnote	`CTRL` + `F7`
Format	`SHIFT` + `F8`
GoTo (Home)	`CTRL` + `7 HOME`
Graphics	`ALT` , `F9`
Hard Page	`CTRL` + `ENTER`

Help	`F3`
Indent from Both L, R Margins	`SHIFT` + `F4`
Indent from Left Margin	`F4`
Insert	`INS`
List Files	`F5`
Macro	`ALT` + `F10`
Macro Def	`CTRL` + `F10`
Margin Release	`SHIFT` + `TAB`
Mark Text	`ALT` + `F5`
Math/Columns	`ALT` + `F7`
Merge	`F9`
Merge Codes	`SHIFT` + `F9`
Merge/Sort	`CTRL` + `F9`
Move Retrieve	`CTRL` + `F4`
Print from Screen	`SHIFT` + `F7`
Pull-Down Menu	`ALT` + `=`
Replace	`ALT` + `F2`
Retrieve Document from Screen	`SHIFT` , `F10`
Reveal Codes	`ALT` + `F3`
	or `F11`
Save/keep on Screen	`F10`
Screen, Rewrite	`CTRL` + `F3`
Screen Down	`+`

Screen Up	`-`
Search Forward	`F2`
Search Backward	`SHIFT` + `F2`
Setup	`SHIFT` + `F1`
Shell (GOTO Dos)	`CTRL` + `F1`
Soft Hyphen	`CTRL` + `-`
Spell	`CTRL` + `F2`
Style	`ALT` + `F8`
Switch	`SHIFT` + `F3`
Tab Align	`CTRL` + `F6`
Text In/Out	`CTRL` + `F5`
Thesaurus	`ALT` + `F1`
Underline	`F8`
Word Left	`CTRL` + `←`
Word Right	`CTRL` + `→`

MERGE CODES

^C   Halt a merge to display a message that allows an entry from the keyboard.

^D   Insert current date into the merged document.

^E   Mark the end of the secondary file record.

^Fn   Indicate a field name or number in a primary file.

^G   Activate a macro.

^N   Look for the next primary file record to continue the merge in progress.

^O   Display the menu, message, instruction, or prompt.

^P   Activate a primary file.

^Q   End a merge.

^R   Mark the end of a field in a secondary file.

^S   Activate a secondary file.

^T   Send merged text to the printer.

^U   Update, rewrite, or view the screen displaying the merge in progress.

^V   Transfer merge codes to a document created by a merge.

HOW TO FORMAT A DISK

1. Insert a DOS diskette into Drive A.
2. Turn on computer.
3. At the prompt, type the current date.
    Press (ENTER).
4. At the prompt, type the current time.
    Press (ENTER).
5. Type Format A: for a one-drive system or
    Format B: for a two-drive system.
    Press (ENTER).
6. Insert a blank diskette into the appropriate drive.
7. Press any key to begin the formatting process.
8. If you want to format another diskette, press (Y)
    for Yes and respond to the prompts on the screen.
    Press (N) for No if you do not want to format
    another diskette.

HOW TO START WORDPERFECT

FLOPPY DISK

1. Place WordPerfect Disk 1 in Drive A.

2. Place a formatted disk in Drive B.

3. Type B: and press (ENTER).

4. Type A:WP and press (ENTER).

HARD DISK

1. At the c:> prompt, type cd\wp50

   At the c:> prompt, type cd\wp51

2. Press (ENTER).

3. Type WP and press (ENTER).

FACTS TO REMEMBER

- Left Margin defaulted at 1".

- Right Margin defaulted at 1".

- Insert mode is defaulted.

- Right justification is on.

Reference Entries:

A to Z

ADVANCE LINE ━━━━━━

NOTE: This advances the printer to a specified line. Use for typing equations, letterheads, etc.

1. Press Shift, F8 (Format).   SHIFT + F8

• *Alt, = Layout; Other.*

2. Press 4 (Other).   4

3. Select option from Advance Menu.

4. Press F7 (Exit).   F7

ALIGN ON TABS ━━━━━━
(Decimal Tab)

1. Press Shift, F8 (Format).   SHIFT + F8

2. Press 1 (Line).   1

3. Press 8 (Tabs).   8

4. Press Home, Home, Left Arrow to   HOME ,

   get to the beginning of the line.   HOME ,

   (NOT NEEDED FOR 5.1)   ←

5. Press Ctrl, End to delete all tabs. CTRL + END

6. Set tab by positioning cursor where tab   D
   should be set and typing "D".

7. Press F7 twice.   F7 , F7

ALIGNMENT CHARACTER (Set) ━━━━━

1. Press Shift, F8 (Format).　　　　　`SHIFT` + `F8`

- *Alt, = Layout, Other.*

2. Press 4 (Other).　　　　　　　　　　`4`

3. Press 3 (Decimal/Align Character).　`3`

4. Type character to be used for aligning text: period (.), comma (,), colon (:), equal sign (=).

    NOTE: Default is the decimal point or period.

5. Press F7 (Exit).　　　　　　　　　　`F7`

APPEARANCE ATTRIBUTES ━━━━━

1. Press Ctrl, F8 (Font).　　　　　　　`CTRL` + `F8`

- *Alt, = Font.*

2. Press 2 (Appearance).　　　　　　　`2`

3. Select Bold, Underline, Double Underline, Italic, Outline, Shadow, SmCap, Extra Large Print, Fine Print, and Large Print Fonts, Redline, or Strikeout.

4. Type text.   INPUT
5. Press Ctrl, F8.   `CTRL` + `F8`
6. Press 3 (Normal).   `3`

AUTOMATIC FORMAT AND REWRITE ════════

1. Press Shift, F1 (Setup).   `SHIFT` + `F1`
- *Alt, =; File; Setup; Display.*
2. Press 3 (Display).   `3`
    Press 2 (Display).   `2`
    Press 6 (Edit-Screen Options).   `6`
3. Press 1 (Automatically Format and Rewrite).   `1`
4. Type Y.   `Y`

AUTOMATIC PAGE NUMBERING ════════

1. Place cursor where page number is desired.
2. Press Ctrl, B.   `CTRL` + `B`
3. Press F7 (Exit).   `F7`

AUTOMATIC REFERENCE ━━━━━━━━━

1. Press Alt, F5 (Mark Text).   `ALT` + `F5`
2. Press 1 (Auto Ref).   `1`
3. Press 1 (Mark Ref).   `1`
4. Select item from menu.

AUXILIARY FILES LOCATION ━━━━━━━━━

1. Press Shift, F1 (Setup).   `SHIFT` + `F1`

• *Alt, =; File; Setup; Location of Files.*

2. Press 7 (Auxiliary Files).   `7`
    Press 6 (Location of Files).   `6`
3. Select item from menu.

BACKUP ━━━━━━━━━━━━━━━━

1. Press Shift, F1 (Setup).   `SHIFT` + `F1`

• *Alt, =; File; Setup; Environment.*

2.   Press 1 (Backup).   ①

    Press 3 (Environment).   ③

    Press 1 (Backup).   ①

3.   Select item from menu.

BASE FONT ───────

1.   Press Ctrl, F8 (Font).   CTRL + F8

-   *Alt, =; Font.*

2.   Press 4 (Base Font).   ④

3.   Select item from menu.

BINDING ───────

> *NOTE: Binding provides for an extra margin along the inside edge of the paper for binding the final copy.*

1.   Press Shift, F7 (Print).   SHIFT + F7

-   *Alt, =; File; Print*

2.   Press B (Binding).   Ⓑ

3.   Type the amount of binding width needed.   INPUT

4.   Press Enter.   ENTER

BLOCK ════════════════════

1. Press Alt, F4, or F12 (Block).   `ALT` + `F4`
                                          or `F12`

- *Alt, =; Edit; Block.*

2. At the bottom left corner of your screen,
    the word "block" will flash off and on.

3. You can now highlight a word,
    sentence, paragraph, or page and
    delete, move, center, or copy the block.

BLOCK APPEND ════════════

1. Place cursor under first character to be
    copied to another document.

- *Alt, =; Edit; Select.*

2. Press Alt, F4, or F12 (Block).   `ALT` + `F4`
                                          or `F12`

3. Highlight text to be copied.

4. Press Ctrl, F4 (Move).   `CTRL` + `F4`

5. Press 1 (Block).   `1`

6. Press 4 (Append).   `4`

7. Message at bottom left corner of your
    screen reads "Append to:".

8. Type name of document that text will   INPUT
    be copied to.

9. Press Enter.   `ENTER`

10. Press F7 (Exit/Save).   `F7`

11. Recall document to which text was   INPUT
    appended.

12. Go to the end of the document to see
    that the text has been copied.

13. Press F7 (Exit).   `F7`

BLOCK PROTECT ━━━━━

1. Place cursor under first character in
    block.

2. Press Alt, F4, or F12 (Block).   `ALT` + `F4`
                                          or `F12`

3. Highlight block to be protected.

4. Press Shift, F8 (Format).   `SHIFT` + `F8`

5. Message reads "Protect Block? (Y/N)".

6. Press Y.   `Y`

BOLD PRINT ━━━━━━━━━━

BEFORE TEXT IS TYPED
1. Press F6. `F6`
2. Type text. INPUT
3. Press F6. `F6`

AFTER TEXT IS TYPED
1. Place cursor under first character of text to be bold printed.
2. Press Alt, F4, or F12 (Block On). `ALT` + `F4`
   or `F12`
3. Highlight text.
4. Press F6. `F6`

CANCEL ━━━━━━━━━━

1. Press F1. `F1`

CANCEL PRINT JOB ━━━━━━

1. Press Shift, F7. `SHIFT` + `F7`
2. Press 4 (Control Printer). `4`
3. Press 1 (Cancel Job/s). `1`

CARTRIDGES AND FONTS ━━━━━

1. Press Shift, F7 (Print).   `SHIFT` + `F7`

   • *Alt, =; File; Print.*

2. Press S (Select Printer).   `S`

3. Press 3 (Edit).   `3`

4. Press 5 (Cartridges and Fonts).   `5`

   Press 4 (Cartridges and Fonts).   `4`

CASE CONVERSION ━━━━━

1. Place cursor on the first character of text
    to be changed to upper/lower case.

   • *Alt, =; Edit; Convert Case.*

2. Press Alt, F4, or F12 (Block).   `ALT` + `F4`
                                              or `F12`

3. Highlight text.

4. Press Shift, F3 (Switch).   `SHIFT` + `F3`

5. Select 1 for uppercase or   `1` *or* `2`
    2 for lowercase.

CENTER

BEFORE TEXT IS TYPED
1. Press Shift, F6 (Center).   `SHIFT` + `F6`

• *Alt, =; Layout; Align; Center*

2. Type text.   INPUT
3. Press Enter.   `ENTER`

AFTER TEXT IS TYPED
1. Place cursor under first character of
    text to be centered.

• *Alt, =; Layout; Align; Center.*

2. Press Alt, F4, or F12 (Block On).   `ALT` + `F4`
                                                 or `F12`

3. Highlight text.
4. Press Shift, F6 (Center).   `SHIFT` + `F6`
5. Press Y.   `Y`

CENTER — DELETE

1. Press Alt, F3, or F11 (Reveal   `ALT` + `F3`
    Codes).   *or* `F11`

2. Highlight the Cntr Code.
3. Press Delete.   `DELETE`

CENTER PAGE ═══════
(Top/Bottom)

1. Place cursor at top of page; line one, position one.

- *Alt, =; Layout; Page.*

2. Press Shift, F8 (Format). `SHIFT` + `F8`
3. Press 2 (Page). `2`
4. Press 1. `1`
5. Press F7 (Exit). `F7`

CHANGE DEFAULT
DIRECTORY ═══════

1. Press F5 (Directory). `F5`
2. Press equal sign. `=`
3. Type name of new directory. INPUT
4. Press Enter. `ENTER`

CHARACTER
REPEAT ══════════════════

*NOTE: The Escape Key is not used to
cancel a requested function. It is used to
cause data to be repeated a particular
number of times.*

1. Press Esc.   `ESC`

2. Message reads "n = 8."

    *NOTE: If you want a character to be
    repeated more than 8 times, strikeover
    the number 8 with another number.*

3. Type the key you want repeated.   INPUT

CLEAR SCREEN
WITHOUT SAVING ════════════

1. Press F7 (Exit).   `F7`

2. Message at bottom reads "Save (Y/N)".

3. Press N.   `N`

4. Message at bottom reads "Exit WP (Y/N)".

5. Press N.   `N`

COLUMN DISPLAY ━━━━━
(Text)

*NOTE: One column displays on the
screen at a time.*

1. Press Shift, F1 (Setup).	`SHIFT` + `F1`
2. Press 3 (Display).	`3`
Press 2 (Display).	`2`
Press 6 (Edit-Screen Options).	`6`
3. Press 8 (Side-by-Side Columns).	`8`
Press 7 (Side-by-Side Columns).	`7`
4. Press Y.	`Y`
5. Press F7 (Exit).	`F7`

COLUMN OFF/ON ━━━━━

1. Press Alt, F7.	`ALT` + `F7`
• *Alt, = Layout; Column; Off.*	
2. Press 3.	`3`
Press 1 (Column).	`1`
Press 1 (On), 2 (Off).	`1` or `2`

COMPOSE — SPECIAL CHARACTERS ════

NOTE: Special characters are fractions, bullets, etc.

1. Press Ctrl, V.   `CTRL` + `V`

    NOTE: Ctrl, V will provide a visible feedback from the editing screen. Ctrl, 2 does not give a visible feedback.

• *Alt, = Font; Characters.*

2. Type characters needed to produce a   INPUT
    special character. Refer to the Word-
    Perfect manual for more information.

CONCORDANCE FILE SETUP ════

1. Begin with a blank screen.

2. Type text to be indexed.   INPUT

3. Repeat step 2 until all text is entered.

4. Press F10 (Save).   `F10`

5. Name the file.   INPUT

6. Press F7 (Exit).   `F7`

CONDITIONAL END OF PAGE
(Page Break)

1. Move cursor to the line immediately above the text you want to stay together.

- *Alt, = Layout; Other.*

2. Press Shift, F8 (Format). `SHIFT` + `F8`

3. Press 4 (Other). `4`

4. Press 2 (Conditional End of Page). `2`

5. Type the number of lines you want kept together. INPUT

6. Press Enter. `ENTER`

7. Press F7 (Exit). `F7`

CONVERT TEXT
(5.1 only)

1. Start at the WP51 directory C:\WP51

2. Type CONVERT. INPUT

3. Press Enter. `ENTER`

4. Type input and output filenames. INPUT

5. Make selection from menu.

COPY ═══════════════════════

1. Place cursor under first character of
    text to be copied.
2. Press Ctrl, F4 (Copy).   `CTRL` + `F4`
3. Press 1 for sentence, 2 for para-   `1` , `2` ,
    graph, 3 for page, or 4 for retrieve.   `3` *or* `4`
4. Press 2 (Copy).   `2`
5. Move cursor to new location.
6. Press Enter.   `ENTER`

COPY/CUT BLOCK ═══════════

1. Place cursor under first character of
    text to be copied.

• *Alt, =; Edit; Block.*

2. Press Alt, F4, or F12 (Block).   `ALT` + `F4`
                                               or `F12`
3. Highlight text.
4. Press Ctrl, F4.   `CTRL` + `F4`
5. Press 1 (Block).   `1`

6. Press 2 (Copy).   ⬚2

7. Move cursor to the new location.

8. Press Enter.   ENTER

COPY/MOVE COLUMN (MATH)

1. Place cursor under first character of text to be moved.

2. Press Alt, F4, or F12 (Block).   ALT + F4

                                                 or F12

3. Highlight text by pressing right and down arrows (all lines will be highlighted).

4. Press Ctrl, F4 (Move).   CTRL + F4

5. Press 2 (Tabular Column).   ⬚2

6. Press 2 (Copy).

7. Place cursor immediately after the first number in the column where you want the column to be copied to.

8. Press Enter.   ENTER

COPY FILE

1. Press F5 (List Files), then Enter if file is
   in the defaulted directory.

   <kbd>F5</kbd> , <kbd>ENTER</kbd>

• *Alt, =; File, List Files.*

2. Enter correct directory if file is not in
   current directory.

   INPUT

3. Select file.

4. Press 8 (Copy).

   <kbd>8</kbd>

5. Type filename with directory if file is to
   be copied to another directory.

   INPUT

6. Press Enter, then 1.

   <kbd>ENTER</kbd> , <kbd>1</kbd>

DATE

1. Position the cursor where you want the
   date to appear.

• *Alt, = Tools; Date Code/Text.*

2. Press Shift, F5.

   <kbd>SHIFT</kbd> + <kbd>F5</kbd>

3. Press 1 (Date).

   <kbd>1</kbd>

DATE FORMAT ━━━━━━━━━

1. Press Shilt, F5 (Date/Outline).   `SHIFT` + `F5`

• *Alt, =, Tools; Date Format.*

2. Press 3 (Date Format).   `3`

3. Select the way you want the date to appear.

4. Press Enter.   `ENTER`

DELETE ━━━━━━━━━━━

NOTE: This entry contains fourteen sub-entries for the following types of deletions: Block, Code, Column, End of Line, End of Page, File, Global, Hard Return, Left (Single Character), Paragraph, Redline/Strike-out, Right (Single Character), Sentence, and Word.

DELETE BLOCK

1. Press Alt, F4, or F12 (Block).   `ALT` + `F4`
    or `F12`

• *Alt, =; Edit; Block.*

2. Highlight text to be deleted.

3. Press Delete.   `DELETE`

4. Prompt reads "Delete Block? (Y/N) N".

5. Press Y.   `Y`

DELETE CODES
*NOTE: Codes are center, outline, tab,
and underline.*

1. Press Alt, F3, or F11   `ALT` + `F3`

   (Reveal Codes).   *or* `F11`

2. Place cursor on the code word.

3. Press Delete.   `DELETE`

DELETE COLUMN
1. Place cursor under first number of
    column to be deleted.

2. Press Alt, F4, or F12 (Block).   `ALT` + `F4`

                                               or `F12`

3. Highlight column using right and down
    cursors (all lines will be highlighted).

4. Press Ctrl, F4 (Move).   `CTRL` + `F4`

5. Press 2 (Tabular Column).   `2`

6. Press 3 (Delete).   `3`

DELETE END OF LINE
1. Place cursor under first character of
    line to be deleted.

2. Press Ctrl, End.   `CTRL` + `END`

DELETE END OF PAGE
1. Place cursor under first character on the page to be deleted.
2. Press Ctrl, Pgdn.   `CTRL` + `PGDN`
3. Type Y.   `Y`

DELETE FILE
1. Press F5 (List Files).   `F5`
2. Type drive name such as A:\.   INPUT
3. Press Enter.   `ENTER`
4. Highlight file to be deleted.
5. Press 2 (Delete).   `2`
6. Prompt reads "Delete...? (Y/N) N".
7. Press Y.   `Y`
8. Press F1 (Exit).   `F1`

DELETE — GLOBAL
1. Place cursor on page one, line one, position one.

• *Alt, =, Search; Replace.*

2. Press Alt, F2 (Replace).   `ALT` + `F2`
3. Press N (Do Not Confirm).   `N`
4. Type text or codes to be deleted.   INPUT
5. Press Alt, F2 (Replace).   `ALT` + `F2`
6. Message reads "Replace with:"
7. Type replacement word.   INPUT

8. Press Alt, F2 (Replace).   [ALT] + [F2]

    *NOTE: Look at document carefully after
    Global Delete as the function may not
    perform exactly as you want.*

DELETE HARD RETURN
1. Press Alt, F3, or F11   [ALT] + [F3]

    (Reveal Codes).   *or* [F11]

2. Place cursor under the Hard Return
    code [HRt].

3. Press Delete.   [DELETE]

DELETE LEFT (Single Character)
1. Place cursor under the character
    immediately after the character to be
    deleted.

2. Press Backspace.   [BACKSPACE]

DELETE PARAGRAPH
1. Place cursor under first character of
    paragraph to be deleted.

2. Press Alt, F4, or F12 (Block).   [ALT] + [F4]

                                        or [F12]

3. Press Enter.   [ENTER]

4. Paragraph is now highlighted.

5. Press Delete.   [DELETE]

6. Prompt reads "Delete Block? (Y/N) N".

7. Press Y.   [Y]

DELETE REDLINE/STRIKEOUT
1.   Place cursor under first character in the
     redline/strikeout area.

2.   Press Backspace.   (BACKSPACE)

DELETE RIGHT (SINGLE CHARACTER)
1.   Place cursor under the character to be
     deleted.

2.   Press Delete.   (DELETE)

DELETE SENTENCE
1.   Place cursor under first character of
     sentence to be deleted.

2.   Press Alt, F4, or F12 (Block).   (ALT) + (F4)
                                             or (F12)

3.   Type end punctuation mark.   INPUT

4.   Sentence is now highlighted.

5.   Press Delete.   (DELETE)

6.   Prompt reads "Delete Block? (Y/N) N."

7.   Press Y.   (Y)

DELETE WORD
1.   Place cursor under first character of
     word to be deleted.

2.   Press Ctrl, Backspace. (CTRL) + (BACKSPACE)

DICTIONARY ══════════════

1. Press F7 (Exit) to leave WordPerfect
    and get to DOS.

2. Type SPELL.   INPUT

3. Press Enter.   [ENTER]

4. The Speller Utility Menu appears and
    includes the following entries:

    0   Exit
    1   Change/Create Dictionary
    2   Add words to the dictionary
    3   Delete words from the dictionary
    4   Optimize dictionary
    5   Display common word list
    6   Check location of a word
    7   Look up
    8   Phonetic look up
    9   Convert 4.2 Dictionary to 5.0
    A   Combine other 5.0 or 5.1 dictionary.
    B   Compress/Expand supplemental dictionary.
    C   Extract added words from wordlist-based dictionary.

5. Make your selection.   INPUT

6. Type filename.   INPUT

7. Press Enter.   [ENTER]

DIRECTORY ══════════════

1. Press F5 (List Files).   [F5]

* *Alt, = Edit; Reveal Codes.*

DISPLAY (REVEAL) CODES ━━━━━━

1. Place cursor at position where you want to see codes.

• *Alt, =; Edit; Reveal Codes.*

2. Press Alt, F3, or F11 (Reveal Codes).

$\boxed{\text{ALT}} + \boxed{\text{F3}}$

or $\boxed{\text{F11}}$

3. Press Alt, F3 to turn off codes.

$\boxed{\text{ALT}} + \boxed{\text{F3}}$

DISPLAY PRINT JOBS ━━━━━

1. Press Shift, F4.

$\boxed{\text{SHIFT}} + \boxed{\text{F7}}$

• *Alt, =; File; Print.*

2. Press 4 (Control Printer).

$\boxed{4}$

3. Press 3 (Display Jobs).

$\boxed{3}$

DISPLAY SETUP ══════

1. Press Shift, F1 (Setup).   (SHIFT) + (F1)

•   *Alt, = File; Setup; Display.*

2. Press 3 (Display).   (3)

    Press 2 (Display).   (2)

3. Select item from menu.   INPUT

4. Press F7 (Exit).   (F7)

DOCUMENT
COMMENT ══════

1. Press Ctrl, F5.   (CTRL) + (F5)

•   *Alt, =; Edit; Comment.*

2. Press 5 (Comment).   (5)

    Press 4 (Comment).   (4)

3. Select item from menu.   INPUT

4. Press F7 (Exit).   (F7)

    *NOTE: The comment will appear on the
    screen but will not print out.*

DOCUMENT SUMMARY

1. Press Shift, F8 (Format). SHIFT + F8

- *Alt, =; File; Summary.*

2. Press 3 (Document). 3
3. Press 5 (Summary). 5
4. Select item(s) to fill in such as author or typist. INPUT
5. Press F7 (Exit). F7

DOUBLE UNDERLINE

1. Press Ctrl, F8 (Font). CTRL + F8
2. Press 2 (Appearance). 2
3. Press 3 (Dbl Und). 3
4. Type text. INPUT
5. Press Ctrl, F8. CTRL + F8
6. Press 3 (Normal). 3

END OF LINE

1. Press End. END

ENDNOTES ━━━━━━━━━━

1. Place cursor where Endnote is to appear.

• *Alt, =; Layout; Endnote.*

2. Press Ctrl, F7 (Footnote). $\boxed{\text{CTRL}}$ + $\boxed{\text{F7}}$

3. Press 2 (Endnote). $\boxed{2}$

4. Press 1 (Create). $\boxed{1}$

5. Press tab once or the spacebar $\boxed{\text{TAB}}$ *or*

    twice to separate number and $\boxed{\text{SPACEBAR}}$

    period from the text you will type. $\boxed{\text{SPACEBAR}}$

6. Type text.   INPUT

7. Press F7 (Exit). $\boxed{\text{F7}}$

ENVELOPE SETUP ━━━━━━━

1. Press Shift, F8 (Format). $\boxed{\text{SHIFT}}$ + $\boxed{\text{F8}}$

2. Press 1 (Lines), then $\boxed{1}$, $\boxed{7}$
    press 7 (Margins L/R).

3. Set LM at 4", then press Enter.   INPUT,

                                                          $\boxed{\text{ENTER}}$

4. Set RM at 1", then press Enter twice.   INPUT,

                                            $\boxed{\text{ENTER}}$, $\boxed{\text{ENTER}}$

5. Press 2 (Page).   ②

6. Press 5 (Top/Bottom Margin).   ⑤

7. Set top margin at 2", then press Enter.   INPUT,

                                                                          ⌈ENTER⌉

8. Set bottom margin at .25", then press   INPUT,

    Enter twice.   ⌈ENTER⌉ , ⌈ENTER⌉

9. Press 8 (Page/Paper Size).   ⑧

    Press 7 (Page/Paper Size).   ⑦

    Press 2 (Add).   ②

    Press 5 (Envelope).   ⑤

    Press 1 (Paper Size).   ①

    Press 5 (Envelope).   ⑤

    Press F7 (Exit), then press 1 (Select).   ⌈F7⌉ , ①

10. Press 5 (Envelope). (5.0 only).   ⑤

11. Press 5 (Envelope). (5.0 only)   ⑤

12. Press F7 (Exit).   ⌈F7⌉

EXTRA LARGE PRINT ━━━━

1. Press Ctrl, F8 (Font).   ⌈CTRL⌉ + ⌈F8⌉

•   *Alt, =; Font; Extra Large.*

2. Press 1 (Size).   ①

3. Press 7 (Extra Large).   7

4. Type text.   INPUT

5. Press Ctrl, F8 (Font).   CTRL + F8

6. Press 3 (Normal).   3

EXIT WP ══════════════
(Exit Word Processing)

1. Press F7 (Exit).   F7

•   *Alt, =; File.*

2. Press Y (Save) or N (No).   Y *or* N

3. Type Document name, or press   INPUT *or*

    Enter if the document has already   ENTER
    been saved.

4. Press Y (Replace) if document has   Y
    already been saved.

5. Press Y (Exit) and the > prompt appears.   Y

FILENAME ON STATUS LINE ━━━━━━━

1. Press Shift, F1 (Setup).   `SHIFT` + `F1`
   - *Alt, =; File; Setup; Display.*
2. Press 3 (Display).   `3`
   Press 2 (Display).   `2`
   Press 6 (Edit Screen Option).   `6`
3. Press 4 (Filename on Status Line).   `4`
   Press 3 (Filename on Status Line).   `3`
4. Press Y, then press Enter.   `Y` , `ENTER`
5. Press F7 (Exit).   `F7`

FINE PRINT ━━━━━━━━━━━

1. Press Ctrl, F8 (Font).   `CTRL` + `F8`
   - *Alt, =; Font; Fine.*
2. Press 1 (Size).   `1`
3. Press 3 (Fine).   `3`
4. Type text.   INPUT
5. Press Ctrl, F8 (Font).   `CTRL` + `F8`
6. Press 3 (Normal).   `3`

FLUSH RIGHT ━━━━━━━━━━━━

1. Move the cursor to the left margin.
2. Press Alt, F6 (Flush Right).   `ALT` + `F6`
3. Type the text, then press Enter.   INPUT ,

                                          `ENTER`

FONTS ━━━━━━━━━━━━━━━━━

1. Press Ctrl, F8 (Fonts).   `CTRL` + `F8`

•   *Alt, =; Fonts.*

2. Make selection.

FOOTERS ━━━━━━━━━━━━━━

1. Place cursor anywhere on Page 1.
2. Press Shift, F8 (Format).   `SHIFT` + `F8`
3. Press 2 (Page).   `2`
4. Press 4 (Footers).   `4`
5. Press 1 (Footer A).   `1`
6. Press 2 (Every Page).   `2`

7. Type text for Footer.   INPUT

    *NOTE: Automatic page numbering is
    Ctrl, B.*

8. Press F7 twice (Exit).   F7 , F7

9. If page numbering is not needed on page   9
    1, press 9 (Suppress Headers/Footers)

    Press 8 (Suppress)   8

10. Press 1.   1

11. Press F7 (Exit) twice.   F7 , F7

FOOTNOTES ━━━━━━━

1. Place cursor where Footnote is needed.

    Alt, =; Layout; Footnote.

2. Press Ctrl, F7 (Footnote).   CTRL , F7

3. Press 1 (Footnote).   1

4. Press 1 (Create).   1

5. Type footnote information.   INPUT

6. Press F7 (Exit).   F7

    *NOTE: Footnotes are automatically
    numbered. Footnotes will not be seen
    in the document.*

FORCE ODD/EVEN PAGES ━━━━━

1. Press Shift, F8 (Format).   `SHIFT` + `F8`
2. Press 2 (Page).   `2`
3. Press 2 (Force Odd/Even Pages).   `2`
4. Select 1 for Odd and 2 for Even.   `1` or `2`
5. Press F7 (Exit).   `F7`

FORMAT LINE MENU ━━━━━

CHANGING LEFT AND RIGHT MARGINS
1. Place cursor at the beginning of the text
    where margin change is needed.

*   *Alt, =; Layout; Line.*

2. Press Shift, F8 (Format).   `SHIFT` + `F8`
3. Press 1 (Line), then press 7 (Margins). `1`, `7`
4. Type left margin number in inches.   INPUT
5. Press Enter.   `ENTER`
6. Type right margin number in inches.   INPUT
7. Press Enter.   `ENTER`
8. Press F7 (Exit).   `F7`

9. Press Alt, F3, or F11 (Reveal   `ALT` + `F3`
    Codes) to see new margins.   or `F11`

10. Press Alt, F3, or F11 to turn   `ALT` + `F3`
    off codes screen.   or `F11`

CHANGING DEFAULTED TABS
1. Press Shift, F8 (Format).   `SHIFT` + `F8`

• *Alt, =; Layout; Line.*

2. Press 1 (Line), then press 8 (Tabs).   `1` , `8`

3. Press Home, Home, Left Arrow to   `HOME` ,
    get to the beginning of the line.   `HOME` , `←`
    (NOT FOR 5.1.)

4. Press Ctrl, End to delete all L's   `CTRL` + `END`
    from the format line.

5. Move cursor to needed tab setting(s).

6. Press Tab.   `TAB`

7. An "L" will appear. Press F7 (Exit).   `F7`

SETTING VERTICAL LINE SPACING
1. Press Shift, F8 (Format).   `SHIFT` + `F8`

• *Alt, =; Layout; Line.*

2. Press 1 (Line).   `1`

3. Press 6 (Line Spacing).   `6`

4. Type number of desired line spacing.   INPUT

5. Press Enter, then press F7 (Exit).   `ENTER` ,
                                           `F7`

FORMS ══════════════════════

1. Press Shift, F7 (Print).   `SHIFT` + `F7`
2. Press S (Select Printer).   `S`
3. Press 3 (Edit), then press 4 (Forms)   `3` , `4`
    and select Form type.
4. Press F7 (Exit) repeatedly until   `F7`
    document screen appears.

1. Press Shift, F8 (Format), then   `SHIFT` + `F8`
    press 2 (Page).   `2`
•   *Alt, =; Layout; Page.*
2. Press 7 (Paper Size) and highlight   `7`
    Form type.   INPUT
3. Press 1 (Select), then press F7 (Exit).   `1` , `F7`

GO — START PRINTER ══════════

NOTE: Needed for printing envelopes.

1. Press Shift, F7.   `SHIFT` + `F7`
•   *Alt, =; File; Print.*
2. Press 4 (Control Printer).   `4`
3. Press 4 (Go).   `4`

GOTO DOS ━━━━━━━━━━━

1. Press Ctrl, F1.   `CTRL` + `F1`

• *Alt, =; File; GoTo Dos.*

2. Press 1 (Go To Dos).   `1`

GRAPHIC BOX ━━━━━━━━━━

1. Press Alt, F9 (Graphics).   `ALT` + `F9`

• *Alt, =; Graphics*

2. Press 3 (Text Box), then press   `3` ,
   4 (Options).   `4`

3. Select border, outside border, or inside
   border.

4. Press Enter.   `ENTER`

5. Press Alt, F9 (Graphics).   `ALT` + `F9`

6. Press 3, then press 1 (Create).   `3` , `1`

7. Make selections from Definition Menu.

8. Press F7 (Exit).   `F7`

9. Press Shift, F7 (Print).   `SHIFT` + `F7`

10. Press 6 (View).   `6`

GRAPHIC FIGURE BOX ═══════

1. Press Alt, F9 (Graphics).   ⎡ ALT ⎤ + ⎡ F9 ⎤

   • *Alt, =; Graphics.*

2. Press 1 (Figure), then press 4 (Options).   ⎡ 1 ⎤ , ⎡ 4 ⎤

3. There are 9 options. Go through each   ⎡ F7 ⎤
   option carefully. When finished with
   Option Menu, press F7 (Exit).

4. You are now ready to create a box.   ⎡ ALT ⎤ + ⎡ F9 ⎤
   Press ALT, F9 (Graphics).

5. Press 1 (Figure), and again press   ⎡ 1 ⎤ ,
   1 (Create).   ⎡ 1 ⎤

6. Press 1 (Filename).   ⎡ 1 ⎤

7. Type filename of graphic   INPUT
   (e.g., arrow-22.wpg).

8. Press Enter.   ⎡ ENTER ⎤

9. Select other items from the menu.   INPUT

10. Press F7 (Exit).   ⎡ F7 ⎤

GRAPHIC FIGURE EDIT ━━━━━━━

1. Press Alt, F9 (Graphics).   `ALT` + `F9`
2. Press 1 (Figure), then press 2 (Edit).   `1`, `2`
3. Type figure number, then press Enter.   INPUT,
                                               `ENTER`
4. Press 8 (Edit).   `8`
   Press 9 (Edit).   `9`

GRAPHIC LINES ━━━━━━━
(Horizontal/Vertical)

1. Press Alt, F9 (Graphics).   `ALT` + `F9`
   • *Alt, =; Graphics; Lines*
2. Press 5 (Line).   `5`
3. Press 1 for Horizontal or 2 for Vertical.   `1`, `2`
4. Press F7 to accept default settings,   `F7` *or*
   or change settings.   INPUT
5. Press F7 (Exit).   `F7`

GRAPHICS SCREEN TYPE ━━━━━━━

1. Press Shift, F1 (Setup).   `SHIFT` + `F1`

• *Alt, =; File; Setup.*

2. Press 3 (Display).   `3`

   Press 2 (Display).   `2`

3. Press 5 (Graphics Screen Type).   `5`

   Press 2 (Graphics Screen Type).   `2`

4. Highlight choice.

5. Press 1 (Select).   `1`

6. Press F7 (Exit).   `F7`

HARD PAGE BREAK ━━━━━━━

1. Place cursor where you want a page break.

2. Press Ctrl, Enter.   `CTRL` + `ENTER`

HARD RETURN ━━━━━
(Display Character)

1. Press Shift, F1 (Setup).   (SHIFT) + (F1)
2. Press 3 (Display).   (3)
   Press 2 (Display).   (2)
3. Press 6 (Hard Return Display Character).   (6)
   Press 6 (Edit–Screen Options).   (6)
   Press 4 (Hard Return Display Characters).   (4)
4. Press Num Lock.   (NUM LOCK)
5. Hold down Alt, and press 1 and 7   (ALT) +
   on the number pad.   (1) + (7)
6. Press Num Lock.   (NUM LOCK)
7. Press F7 (Exit).   (F7)

HARD SPACE ━━━━━

1. Press Home, Space.   (HOME) +
                                               (SPACEBAR)

HEADERS ━━━━━━━━━━━━

1. Place cursor on the first page.

*   *Alt, =; Layout; Page.*

    NOTE: If first page is not to be numbered, cursor MUST be located after the first line of text.

2. Press Shift, F8 (Format).   (SHIFT) + (F8)

3. Press 2 (Page).   (2)

4. Press 3 (Header).   (3)

5. Press 1 (Header A).   (1)

6. Press 2 (Every Page).   (2)

7. Message at bottom left reads "Press Exit when done."

8. Type Header information.   INPUT

9. Press F7 twice (Exit).   (F7) , (F7)

10. If footers will not be set up at this time, press 9 (Suppress Headers/Footers).   (9)

    Press 8 (Suppress).   (8)

11. Press 1.   (1)

12. Press F7 (exit) twice.   (F7) , (F7)

HELP ━━━━━━━━━━

1. Press F3.   `F3`

•   *Alt, =; Help.*

2. Press Space to exit back to   `SPACEBAR`
    screen.

HYPHENATION ━━━━━━

1. Place cursor at top of the document.

•   *Alt, =; Layout; Page*

2. Press Shift, F8 (Format).   `SHIFT` + `F8`

3. Press 1 (Line).   `1`

4. Press 1 (Hyphenation).   `1`

5. Press 1 for Off, 2 for Manual,   `1` ,

    and 3 for Auto.   `2` *or* `3`

6. Press F7 (Exit).   `F7`

    NOTE: Keep a dictionary close by!
    WordPerfect is not perfect.

HYPHENATION ZONE ━━━━

1. Place cursor at beginning of document.

• *Alt, =; Layout; Line.*

2. Press Shift, F8.   (SHIFT) + (F8)
3. Press 1 (Line).   (1)
4. Press 2 (Hyphenation Zone, L/R).   (2)
5. Type a value for the L zone.   INPUT
6. Press Enter.   (ENTER)
7. Type a value for the R Zone.   INPUT
8. Press Enter.   (ENTER)
9. Press F7 (Exit).   (F7)

INDENT ━━━━━━━

1. Press F4.   (F4)

• *Alt, =; Layout; Align.*

2. Type text.   INPUT
3. Press Enter.   (ENTER)

INDENT FROM LEFT & RIGHT MARGINS ━━━━━

BEFORE TEXT IS TYPED
1. Press Shift, F4.   (SHIFT) + (F4)

•   *Alt, =; Layout; Align.*

2. Type text.   INPUT

3. Press Enter.   (ENTER)

AFTER TEXT IS TYPED
1. Place cursor at left margin.

2. Press Shift, F4.   (SHIFT) + (F4)

3. Press Down Arrow.   (↓)

INDENTS - HANGING ━━━━━

*NOTE: In a hanging indent, the first line
is not indented but remaining lines are.*

1. Press F4 (Indent).   (F4)

•   *Alt, =; Layout; Align.*

2. Press Shift, Tab (Margin Release). (SHIFT)
                                        + (TAB)

3. Type paragraph.   INPUT

4. Press Enter.   (ENTER)

INDEX ══════════════════════

NOTE: This feature creates an alphabetized list of index entries and subentries for a document in three steps.

STEP ONE: Create Index Entries
NOTE: There are two ways to create index entries: A. Mark Text, and B, Concordance.

A. Mark Text
One-word entry
1.   Place cursor anywhere in the word.

* *Alt, =; Mark; Index.*

2.   Press Alt, F5 (Mark Text).   (ALT) + (F5)

3.   Press 3 (Index).   (3)

4.   Press Enter.   (ENTER)

5.   Type a subheading if needed.   INPUT

6.   Press Enter.   (ENTER)

Two or more words
1.   Place cursor at beginning of phrase.

2.   Press Alt, F4, or F12 (Block).   (ALT) + (F4)

                                                              or (F12)

3.   Highlight text to be indexed.

4.   Press Alt, F5 (Mark Text).   (ALT) + (F5)

5.   Press 3 (Index).   (3)

6.   Press Enter.   (ENTER)

7. Type a subheading if needed.   INPUT
8. Press Enter.   `ENTER`

B. Concordance

1. Start with an empty screen.
2. Type the indexed word.   INPUT
3. Press Enter.   `ENTER`
4. Repeat steps 2 and 3 until all entries have been made.

STEP TWO: Define Index

1. To define the index, begin by placing the cursor at the end of the document.
2. Press Ctrl, Enter (Hard Page) to start Index on a separate page.   `CTRL` + `ENTER`
3. Type a heading.   INPUT
4. Press Alt, F5 (Mark Text).   `ALT` + `F5`

• *Alt, =; Mark; Define; Index*

5. Press 5 (Define).   `5`
6. Press 3 (Define Index).   `3`
7. Press Enter if a Mark text index, or type Concordance filename and press Enter.   `ENTER` *or* INPUT , `ENTER`
8. Select page number style.
9. You are now ready to Generate.

STEP THREE: Generate Index

1. To generate the index, place the cursor at the location in the document where the Index is to appear.

2. Press Alt, F5 (Mark Text).   `ALT` + `F5`

   - *Alt, =; Mark; Generate.*

3. Press 6 (Generate).   `6`

4. Press 5 (Generate Tables, Indexes, Automatic References).   `5`

5. Prompt reads "Existing tables lists and indexes will be replaced. Continue (Y/N) Y".

6. Press Y.   `Y`

7. Message reads "Generation in progress." The Counter appears. The table of contents appears in the document where the cursor was located.

8. Press F10 (Save).   `F10`

INITIAL CODES ━━━━━

1. Press Shift, F8 (Format).   `SHIFT` + `F8`

2. Press 3 (Document).   `3`

3. Press 2 (Initial Codes).   `2`

4. Press Shift, F8 (Format).   `SHIFT` + `F8`

5. Make changes in the format menu.   INPUT

6. Press F7 three times to exit.   `F7` , `F7` ,
                                                      `F7`

INSERT

1. Place cursor under first character
   immediately after the insert.

2. Type information.   INPUT

3. Press Down Arrow to adjust line.   `↓`

ITALICS

1. Press Ctrl, F8 (Font).   `CTRL` + `F8`

2. Press 2 (Appearance).   `2`

3. Press 4 (Italic).   `4`

4. Type text.   INPUT

5. Press Ctrl, F8 (Font).   `CTRL` + `F8`

6. Press 3 (Normal).   `3`

JUSTIFICATION

1. Press Shift, F8 (Format).   SHIFT + F8
2. Press 1 (Line).   1
3. Press 3 (Justification).   3
    Select 1 for left, 2 for center,   1 , 2 ,
    3 for right, or 4 for full.   3 or 4
4. Press Y or N.   Y or N
5. Press F7 (Exit).   F7

KERNING

1. Press Shift, F8 (Format).   SHIFT + F8
2. Press 4 (Other).   4
3. Press 6 (Printer Functions).   6
4. Press 1 (Kerning).   1
5. Make changes.   INPUT
6. Press F7 (Exit).   F7

KEYBOARD DIRECTLY TO THE PRINTER ──── (5.0 only)

1. Press Shift, F7 (Print).   `SHIFT` + `F7`
 • *Alt, =; File; Print.*
2. Press 5 (Type-thru).   `5`
3. Press 1 (By Line).   `1`
4. Type text.   INPUT
5. Press Enter. The text will print out.   `ENTER`
6. Repeat steps 4 and 5 for additional
   lines to print from keyboard.

LABELS — MAILING ──── (5.1 only)

1. Press Shift, F8 (Format).   `SHIFT` + `F8`
 • *Alt, =; Layout; Page.*
2. Press 1 (Line).   `1`
3. Press 7 (Margins L/R).   `7`
4. Set LM at zero, then press Enter.   `0` , `ENTER`
5. Set RM at zero, then press Enter.   `0` , `ENTER`

6. Press Esc to go back to the Format menu.   (ESC)

7. Press 2 (Page).   (2)

8. Press 5 (Top/Bottom Margin).   (5)

9. Set top margin at zero, then   (0) ,

   press Enter.   (ENTER)

10. Set bottom margin at zero, then   (0) ,

    press Enter.   (ENTER)

11. Press 7 (Paper Size).   (7)

12. Press 2 (Add).   (2)

13. Press 4 (Labels).   (4)

14. Press 8 (Labels), then press Y.   (8) , (Y)

15. Press 5 (Label Margins).   (5)

16. Set LM at .25, then press Enter.   INPUT ,

                                            (ENTER)

17. Press F7 five (5) times.   (F7) , (F7) ,

                                  (F7) , (F7) , (F7)

18. Highlight label size: "Label, Wide" will show one label at a time on the View Document screen, and "8 1/2 x 11" will show three labels across on the View Document screen.

19. Press 1 (Select).   (1)

20. Press F7 (Exit).   (F7)

21. To center label top/bottom:
    Press Shift, F8 (Format).   `SHIFT` + `F8`

    Press 2 (Page).   `2`

    Press 1, "Y".   `1` , `Y`

    Press F7 (Exit).   `F7`

22. Type label text.   INPUT

23. Press Ctrl, Enter after each   `CTRL` + `ENTER`
    completed label.

24. Repeat steps 20 to 23 for each label.

25. Press F7 (Exit/Save).   `F7`

LABELS — PRINT ────────

1. Place cursor under first character in the
   label to be printed.

2. Press Shift, F7 (Print).   `SHIFT` + `F7`

3. Press 2 (Page).   `2`

4. Repeat steps 1 to 3.

LANGUAGE CODE ━━━━━

NOTE: WordPerfect can check your work for spelling, hyphenation, and thesaurus use for 14 languages.

1. Press Shift, F8 (Format).   `SHIFT` + `F8`
2. Press 4 (Other).   `4`
3. Press 4 (Language).   `4`
4. Type language code.   INPUT
5. Press F7 twice (Exit).   `F7` , `F7`

LARGE PRINT ━━━━━

1. Press Ctrl, F8 (Font).   `CTRL` + `F8`
  • *Alt, =; Font.*
2. Press 1 (Size).   `1`
3. Press 5 (Large).   `5`
4. Type text.   INPUT
5. Press Ctrl, F8 (Font).   `CTRL` + `F8`
6. Press 3 (Normal).   `3`

LEFT MARGIN RELEASE

1. Place cursor at left margin.
2. Press Shift, Tab.   SHIFT + TAB
   The cursor moves left 1 tab position.
3. Type text.   INPUT
4. Press Tab to return to original left margin.   TAB

LINE DRAW

1. Press Ctrl, F3.   CTRL + F3
   - *Alt, =; Tools; Line Draw.*
2. Press 2 (Line Draw).   2
3. Make selection by pressing 1 for Single   1 ,
   Line, 2 for Double Line, 3 for Asterisks,   2 , 3 ,
   4 for Change, 5 for Erase, or 6 for   4 , 5
   Move.   *or* 6
4. Use cursor keys to draw line or box.
5. Press F7 (Exit).   F7

LINE FORMAT ════════════

1. Press Shift, F8 (Format).   `SHIFT` + `F8`

- *Alt, =; Layout; Line.*

2. Press 1 (Line).   `1`

3. Select item to be changed from menu.

LINE HEIGHT ════════════

1. Press Shift, F8 (Line).   `SHIFT` + `F8`

- *Alt, =; Layout; Line.*

2. Press 1 (Line).   `1`

3. Press 4 (Height).   `4`

4. Press 1 for Auto or 2 for Fixed.   `1` *or* `2`

5. Press F7 (Exit).   `F7`

LINE NUMBERING ════════════

1. Place cursor at the beginning of the
    document.

2. Press Shift, F8 (Format Menu).   `SHIFT` + `F8`

- *Alt, =; Layout; Line.*

3. Press 1 (Line). [1]
4. Press 5 (Line Numbering). [5]
5. Press Y. [Y]
6. Press Enter. [ENTER]
7. Press F7 (Exit). [F7]

   NOTE: Line numbering will not be seen on the typing screen. You can see the line numbers before printing by pressing Shift, F7, then 6 (View Document).

LINE SPACING

1. Press Shift, F8 (Format). [SHIFT] + [F8]
- *Alt, =; Layout; Line.*

2. Press 1 (Line). [1]
3. Press 6 (Spacing). [6]
4. Type number. INPUT
5. Press F7 (Exit). [F7]

LISTS ═══════════════════

NOTE: Three functions must be performed to produce a list: Marking, Defining, and Generating.

STEP ONE: Marking Text

1. Place cursor under the first character of the text to be in the list.

2. Press Alt, F4, or F12 (Block). $\boxed{\text{ALT}}$ + $\boxed{\text{F4}}$
   or $\boxed{\text{F12}}$

3. Highlight word(s).

4. Press Alt, F5 (Mark Text). $\boxed{\text{ALT}}$ + $\boxed{\text{F5}}$

5. Press 2 (List). $\boxed{2}$

6. Type number of list (1-10), then   INPUT ,
   press Enter. $\boxed{\text{ENTER}}$

7. Repeat steps 1 to 6 until all words have been marked.

STEP TWO: Define Words

1. Place cursor in the document where the list is to appear.

2. Press Ctrl, Enter to create a $\boxed{\text{CTRL}}$ +
   new page for the list. $\boxed{\text{ENTER}}$

3. Type a title, then press Enter   INPUT ,
   three times. $\boxed{\text{ENTER}}$,
                              $\boxed{\text{ENTER}}$, $\boxed{\text{ENTER}}$

4. Press Alt, F5 (Mark Text). $\boxed{\text{ALT}}$ + $\boxed{\text{F5}}$

5. Press 5 (Define). ⬚ 5

6. Press 2 (List). ⬚ 2

7. Enter number of the desired list (1-10). INPUT

8. Press Enter. ⬚ ENTER

9. Make selection from List Definition Menu.

STEP THREE: Generate

1. Press Alt, F5 (Mark Text). ⬚ ALT + ⬚ F5

2. Press 6 (Generate). ⬚ 6

3. Press 5 (Generate Table, Indexes, etc.). ⬚ 5

4. Press Y. ⬚ Y

LIST (DISPLAY) FILES SAVED/DIRECTORY ▬▬▬

1. Press F5. ⬚ F5

• *Alt, =; File; List Files.*

2. The name of the disk drive that disk is in INPUT
   will be displayed. (EXAMPLE: Dir C:\) If
   drive displayed is not correct, type in correct drive name.

3. Press Enter. ⬚ ENTER

4. Files are displayed. Press F1 (Cancel/ ⬚ F1
   Return to Editing Screen).

LOCKED DOCUMENT ━━━━━
(PASSWORD PROTECT)

1.	Press Ctrl, F5 (Text In/Out).	`CTRL` + `F5`

*   *Alt, =; File; Password.*

2.	Press 2 (Password).	`2`
3.	Press 1 (Add/Change).	`1`
4.	Type password, then press	INPUT ,
	Enter.	`ENTER`
5.	Repeat step 4.	INPUT , `ENTER`
6.	Press F7 (Exit).	`F7`
7.	Press F7 (Exit/Save).	`F7`

LOOK AT A SAVED
DOCUMENT ━━━━━

*NOTE: This allows you to see the file
without bringing it on to the screen.*

1.	Press F5 (List Files).	`F5`
2.	Highlight file, then press 6 (Look).	`6`

MACRO

STEP ONE: Creating a Macro

1. Place cursor where Macro information is to be typed.

- *Alt, =; Tools; Macro; Define.*

2. Press Ctrl, F10 (Macro Def.). $\quad$ `CTRL` + `F10`

3. Prompt reads "Define Macro."

4. Type name of Macro (name can be $\quad$ INPUT ,

   up to 8 characters long), and then $\quad$ `ENTER`
   press Enter.

5. Prompt reads "Description."

6. Type a short description of what the $\quad$ INPUT ,

   Macro does, and then press Enter. $\quad$ `ENTER`

7. "Macro Def" appears at the bottom of the screen.

8. Type the Macro text. $\quad$ INPUT

9. Press Ctrl, F10 (Macro Def). $\quad$ `CTRL` + `F10`

10. Repeat steps 2 to 9.

11. Press F7 (Exit/Save). $\quad$ `F7`

STEP TWO: Editing a Macro

1. Press Ctrl, F10 (Macro Def.). $\quad$ `CTRL` + `F10`

2. Type Macro name, then press Enter. $\quad$ INPUT ,

   $\quad$ `ENTER`

3. Press 2 (Edit). $\quad$ `2`

4.   Make changes.   INPUT

5.   Press F7 (Exit/Save).   (F7)

STEP THREE: Retrieving a Macro

1.   Place cursor where Macro is to be
     printed.

2.   Press Alt, F10.   (ALT) + (F10)

*   *Alt, =; Tools; Macro; Execute.*

3.   Prompt reads "Macro."

4.   Type the name of the Macro, then   INPUT ,
     press Enter.   (ENTER)

MACRO PAUSES ════════════

*NOTE: Macro Pauses allows you to type text, other
than the predefined Macro text, when you are using
a Macro. When you retrieve the Macro, the Macro
will pause at this position so that you may enter the
text.*

1.   Follows steps 1 to 8 in Creating a
     Macro, under the Macro entry.

2.   Place cursor where you want the pause.

3.   Press Ctrl, PgUp (a beep sounds).   (CTRL) +
                                               (PgUp)

4.   Press 1 (Pause).   (1)

5. Type text. (It will not be stored.)   INPUT
6. Press Enter twice.   (ENTER) , (ENTER)
7. Press Ctrl, F10 (Macro Def.).   (CTRL) + (F10)
8. Repeat steps 1 to 7.
9. Press F7 (Exit/Save).   (F7)

MARGINS ───────────────

1. Press Shift, F8 (Format).   (SHIFT) + (F8)
•   *Alt, =; Layout; Line.*
2. Press 1 (Line).   (1)
3. Press 7 (Margins Left/Right).   (1)
4. Type setting for left margin (inches).   INPUT
5. Press Enter.   (ENTER)
6. Type setting for right margin (inches).   INPUT
7. Press Enter.   (ENTER)
8. Press F7 (Exit).   (F7)

MARK TEXT ───────────────

1. Press Alt, F5 (Mark Text).   (ALT) + (F5)
2. Select item from menu.

MATH ━━━━━━━━━━━━━━━━━━

NOTE: The plus operator (Shift, +)
adds subtotals. The equals operator (=)
adds totals.

1. Set aligned tabs (Decimal Tab).   INPUT

2. Press Alt, F7 (Math/Columns).   `ALT` + `F7`

   Press 3 (Math), then press 3 (Define).   `3` , `3`

3. Press 2 (Math Definition Menu).   `2`

• *Alt, =; Layout; Math; On.*

4. The Math Definition Menu shows 24   `0` ,
   columns with headings A-X. Enter the   `1` ,
   type of column with a 0 to 4 as   `2` , `3`
   indicated on the menu.   *or* `4`
   When completed, press F7 (Exit).   `F7`

5. Type 1 (Turn Math On).   `1`

6. Type the table.   INPUT

7. Type "Subtotal". Press Tab to decimal   INPUT ,
   position and type a plus (+).   `TAB` , `+`

8. Press Alt, F7 (Math/Columns).   `ALT` + `F7`

9. Press 2 (Calculate).   `2`

   Press 3 (Math), then press 4 (Calculate).   `3` , `4`

   Answer appears.

10. Continue typing table and calculating
    subtotals by repeating steps 6 to 9.

11. At the total position, press Tab to decimal position, then type an equals (=).   (TAB) , (=)

12. Press Alt, F7 (Math/Column).   (ALT) + (F7)

13. Press 2 (Calculate).   (2)

Press 3 (Math), then press 4 (Calculate).   (3) , (4)

14. When finished with all math calculations, press Alt, F7.   (ALT) + (F7)

15. Press 1 (Math Off).   (1)

Press 3 (Math), then press 2 (Off).   (3) , (2)

• *Alt, =; Layout; Math; Off.*

MATH OPERATORS

*   Adds all the totals derived with the equals (=) operator. Use for Grand Totals.   (SHIFT) + (*)

\+   Adds all numbers in the column.   (SHIFT) , (+)

=   Adds all subtotals and extra subtotals since last total.   (=)

t   Provides for additional subtotals.   (t)

T   Provides for additional totals.   (T)

N   Reverses the sign of the result of number immediately following operator for use in further calculations.   (N)

MERGE ═══════════════

STEP ONE: Create Form Letter/Document

1. Press Shift, F9 (Merge Code) where variable information is to go in document.   `SHIFT` + `F9`

- *Alt, =; Tools; Merge.*

2. Press F (Fields).   `F`

Press 1 (Fields).   `1`

3. Prompt reads "Field Number?"

4. Type 1 (Field 1 represents the first variable in the document).   `1`

5. Press Enter.   `ENTER`

6. Repeat steps 1 to 5, increasing the Field Number each time by 1 for each additional variable.

7. Press F7 (Save and Name File).   `F7`

STEP TWO: Create Variables for Secondary Document

1. Type first variable information.   INPUT

- *Alt, =; Tools; Merge.*

2. Press F9. ^R (End Field) will appear.   `F9`

3. Type other variable information, press-   INPUT ,

   ing F9 at the end of each variable.   `F9`

4. Press Shift, F9 (^E) to end the (SHIFT) + (F9)
    variable information for the document.

    Press 2 (End Record).   (2)

5. Repeat steps 1 to 4 for the next document.

    *NOTE: NEVER OMIT A FIELD IN THE
    SECONDARY DOCUMENT.*

6. Press F7 (Save and Name Variable Files.)   (F7)

    *NOTE: Follow these guidelines when using Fields
    more than once. In the primary document, repeat
    the Field Number whenever variable will be the
    same as in the first case. In the secondary docu-
    ment, you only need to type the Field Number once.*

STEP THREE: Omit If Blank

1. Type a question mark (?) after the Field   INPUT
    Number in the merge code.

    *NOTE: This prevents a blank space from
    occurring if there is no variable for the Field
    Number in the secondary document.*

2. In the secondary document, press F9   (F9)
    (^R) on a line by itself.

MERGE — ENVELOPE
PRIMARY FILE ════════════

*NOTE: Refer to the Envelope entry for steps on
how to set the envelope format. Then proceed with
the following:*

1. Press Shift, F9 (Merge Code).   `SHIFT` + `F9`

2. Press F (Field).   `F`

   Press 1 (Field).   `1`

3. Message reads "Field Number?"

4. Press 1 (Address Field).   `1`

5. Press Enter.   `ENTER`

6. ^F1^ will now be on the screen.

7. Press F7 (Save and Name the   `F7`
   Envelope File).

MERGE FROM KEYBOARD

NOTE: This merge enables you to merge from the keyboard without a secondary document.

1. At position for variables in the Pri-   `CTRL` + `C`
   mary document, press Ctrl, C (^C)   *or*
   (Entry from Console) or Ctrl, D (^D)   `CTRL` + `D`
   (Current Date).

2. At the end of the document, press F7   `F7`
   (Exit/Save).

3. Press Y (Save).   `Y`

4. Press N (Clear Screen).   `N`

MERGE VARIABLE SETUP AT KEYBOARD

1. Press Ctrl, F9 (Merge). `CTRL` + `F9`

2. Press 1 (Merge). `1`

3. Type Primary document name. INPUT

4. Press Enter. `ENTER`

5. There is no Secondary document `ENTER`
   name, so press Enter.

6. "Merging" appears on the status line.

7. The first ^C is not seen. Type the INPUT
   variable text.

8. Press F9 (Merge Return). `F9`

9. The cursor will move to the next ^C INPUT
   position. Type the text.

10. Repeat steps 6 to 9.

11. When the merging is finished, "Merging" will disap-
    pear from the screen. The document can now be
    saved and printed.

MERGE PRINT
(Document/Variables)

1. Press Ctrl, F9 (Merge/Sort). `CTRL` + `F9`

2. Press 1 (Merge). `1`

3. Prompt reads "Primary file:".

4. Type name of letter/document file.   INPUT

5. Press Enter.   (ENTER)

6. Prompt reads "Secondary file:".

7. Type name of secondary file.   INPUT

8. Press Enter.   (ENTER)

9. Message reads "Merge". When merging is finished, the cursor will appear on the screen after the last letter.

10. Press Home, Home, Up Arrow.   (HOME), (HOME), (↑)

11. First letter/document will appear on the screen.

12. Press Shift, F7 (Print).   (SHIFT) + (F7)

13. Press 1.   (1)

MERGE-PRINT ENVELOPES

1. Press Ctrl, F9 (Merge/Sort).   (CTRL) + (F9)

2. Press 1 (Merge).   (1)

3. Type name of envelope (Primary file).   INPUT

4. Press Enter.   (ENTER)

5. Type name of variable (Secondary file).   INPUT

6. Press Enter. Addresses will appear on the screen with a page break between each one.   (ENTER)

7. Place envelope in printer.

8. Place cursor under the first character in the address to be printed.

9.   Press Shift, F7 (Print).   `SHIFT` + `F7`

10. Press 2 (Page). You may hear a beep.   `2`

11. Press Shift, F7 (Print).   `SHIFT` , `F7`

12. Press 4 (Control Printer).   `4`

13. Press G (Go).   `G`

14. Repeat steps 7 to 13.

15. Press F7 (Exit).   `F7`

MERGE-DIRECT TO PRINTER

1.   At the end of the primary   `SHIFT` + `F9`

     document, press Shift, F9 (Merge Code).

2.   Type Ctrl, T, then Ctrl, N, then   `CTRL` + `T` ,

     Ctrl, P twice.   `CTRL` + `N` ,

     `CTRL` + `P` , `CTRL` + `P`

     T   Sends to printer any text merged to this point.
     N   Fetches next record in secondary file.
     P   Primary File.
     P   Primary File.

3.   When ready to print the   `CTRL` + `F9`
     Merge File, press Ctrl, F9.

4.   Press 1 (Merge).   `1`

5.   Type Primary document name.   INPUT

6.   Press Enter.   `ENTER`

7.   Type Secondary document name.   INPUT

8.   "Merging" appears on the status line. Merge File
     goes directly to the printer, and the screen is blank.

MOUSE SETUP
(5.1 only)

1. Press Shift, F1 (Setup).   `SHIFT` + `F1`
- *Alt, =; File; Setup.*
2. Press 1 (Mouse).   `1`
3. Make selection(s).   INPUT
4. Press F7 (Exit).   `F7`

MOVE

1. Place cursor under the first character to be moved.
- *Alt, =; Edit; Select.*
2. Press Ctrl, F4 (Move).   `CTRL` + `F4`
3. Press 1 for Sentence, 2 for Paragraph, `1`, `2`,
   3 for Page, or 4 for Retrieve.   `3` *or* `4`
4. Press 1 (Move).   `1`
5. Move cursor to the new location.
6. Press Enter.   `ENTER`

MOVE — BLOCK
1. Place cursor under first character to be moved.
- *Alt, =; Edit; Select; Rectangle or Tabular Column.*

2. Press Alt, F4, or F12 (Block).   `ALT` + `F4`
                                                       or `F12`

3. Highlight text to be moved.

4. Press Ctrl, F4 (Move).   `CTRL` + `F4`

5. Press 1 (Block).   `1`

6. Press 1 (Move).   `1`

7. Move cursor to new location for text.

8. Press Enter.   `ENTER`

MOVE/COPY TEXT FROM ONE DOCUMENT TO ANOTHER

1. The document to receive the moved text should be on the screen.

2. Press Shift, F3 (Switch Key).   `SHIFT` + `F3`

3. The screen is blank. You are now in Doc 2, Pg 1.

4. To retrieve the document with the text to be moved, follow these steps:

   Press Shift, F10.   `SHIFT` + `F10`

   Type filename.   INPUT

   Press Enter.   `ENTER`

5. Place the cursor under the first character to be moved.

6. Press Alt, F4, or F12 (Block).   `ALT` + `F4`
                                                       or `F12`

7. Highlight the text to be moved.

8. Press Ctrl, F4 (Move). $\boxed{CTRL} + \boxed{F4}$

9. Press 1 (Block). $\boxed{1}$

10. Press 1 for (Move), or 2 for (Copy). $\boxed{1}$ *or* $\boxed{2}$

11. Press Shift, F3 (Switch Key). $\boxed{SHIFT} + \boxed{F3}$

12. Position the cursor to where the text is
    to be moved or copied.

13. Press Enter. $\boxed{ENTER}$

14. Press F7 to exit from each document. $\boxed{F7}$

NAME DOCUMENT

1. Press F7 (Exit). $\boxed{F7}$

• *Alt, =; File; Save.*

2. Message reads "Save Document? (Y/N) Y".

3. Press Y. $\boxed{Y}$

4. Prompt reads "Document to be saved:"

5. Type a filename up to 8 characters.   INPUT
    Do not use any blank spaces.

6. Press Enter. $\boxed{ENTER}$

NEW PAGE (Hard Page)

1. Press Ctrl, Enter where you want a new page. $\boxed{\text{CTRL}} + \boxed{\text{ENTER}}$

NEW PAGE/PAPER SIZE

1. Press Shift, F8 (Format). $\boxed{\text{SHIFT}} + \boxed{\text{F8}}$

- *Alt, =; Layout; Page.*

2. Press 2 (Page). $\boxed{2}$

3. Press 8 (Paper Size). $\boxed{8}$

   Press 7 (Paper Size). $\boxed{7}$

4. Make selection from menu.   INPUT

5. Make selection from menu again.   INPUT

   Press 1 (Select). $\boxed{1}$

6. Press F7 (Exit). $\boxed{\text{F7}}$

NEWSPAPER COLUMNS

1. Press Alt, F7 (Math/Columns).   `ALT` + `F7`

   • *Alt, =; Layout; Columns.*

2. Press 4 (Column Define).   `4`

   Press 1 (Column).   `1`

   Press 3 (Define).   `3`

3. Press 2 (Number of Columns).   `2`

4. Type number of columns, then press   INPUT ,

   Enter.   `ENTER`

5. Press 3 (Distance between Columns).   `3`

6. Type in amount of space between   INPUT

   columns, or press Enter to accept the   `ENTER`
   default setting.

7. In most cases, you can accept the default
   settings for margins OR to change margins
   Press 4 (Margins).   `4`

8. Key the desired margins pressing   INPUT

   Enter after each one.   `ENTER`

9. Press 3 (Column On/Off).   `3`

   Press 1 (Column On).   `1`

10. Type text.   INPUT

11. Press Alt, F7.   `ALT` + `F7`

12. Press 3 (Column On/Off).   3

• *Alt, =; Layout; Columns; Off.*

Press 1 (Column).   1

Press 2 (Off).   2

EDITING NEWSPAPER COLUMNS
NOTE: This will move the cursor from one column to another.

1. Press Ctrl, Home.   (CTRL) + (HOME)

2. Message reads "Go to".

3. Press Right Arrow or Left Arrow.   (→)

   Cursor will move to another column.   *or* (←)

COLUMN DISPLAY FOR EFFICIENT EDITING
NOTE: Displaying only one column on a page makes for easier editing.

1. Press Shift, F8 (Format).   (SHIFT) + (F8)

2. Press 3 (Display).   3

   Press 2 (Display).   2

   Press 6 (Edit Screen Options).   6

3. Press 8 (Side by Side Columns).   8

   Press 7 (Side-by-Side Columns).   7

4. Press N.   N

5. Press F7 (Exit).   F7

NUMBER OF COPIES ═══

1. Press Shift, F7 (Print). $\boxed{\text{SHIFT}} + \boxed{\text{F7}}$
2. Press N (Number of Copies). $\boxed{\text{N}}$
3. Type number of copies needed.   INPUT
4. Press Enter. $\boxed{\text{ENTER}}$
5. Press 1 (Full Text) to print. $\boxed{1}$

OUTLINE ═══

1. Press Shift, F5 (Date/Outline). $\boxed{\text{SHIFT}} + \boxed{\text{F5}}$

• *Alt, =; Tools; Outline.*

2. Press 4 (Outline). $\boxed{4}$
3. Press Enter. The Roman numeral I $\boxed{\text{ENTER}}$
   is displayed.

   Press 1 (On), then press Enter. $\boxed{1}$, $\boxed{\text{ENTER}}$

4. Press F4 (Indent). $\boxed{4}$
5. Type text for this level.   INPUT
6. Press Enter. The Roman numeral II $\boxed{\text{ENTER}}$
   is displayed.
7. Press Tab. The letter A appears. $\boxed{\text{TAB}}$
8. Press F4 (Indent). $\boxed{\text{F4}}$
9. Type information, then press Enter. $\boxed{\text{ENTER}}$

10. Press Tab. The letter B is displayed.   `TAB`

11. Press F4 (Indent).   `F4`

12. Continue typing the outline   `SHIFT` + `TAB`
    repeating steps 9 to 11. Press
    Shift, Tab to change para-
    graph number.

13. Press Shift, F5 to end.   `SHIFT` + `F5`

14. Press 4 to turn Outline Off.   `4`

    Press 2 (Off).   `2`

• *Alt, =; Tools; Outline.*

PAGE FORMAT ─────

1. Press Shift, F8 (Format).   `SHIFT` + `F8`

• *Alt, =; Layout; Page.*

2. Press 2 (Page).   `2`

3. You can now change the top margin,
   page length, and page numbering.

PAGE NUMBERING ─────

1. Place the cursor at the top of the document.

• *Alt, =; Layout; Page.*

2. Press Shift, F8 (Format). `SHIFT` + `F8`

3. Type 2 (Page). `2`

4. Press 6 (New Page Number). `6`

5. Type new number, and make selection. INPUT

6. Press Enter. `ENTER`

7. Press F7 (Exit). `F7`

AUTOMATIC PAGE NUMBERING IN A FOOTER

1. Place the cursor on the first page of the document.

2. Press Shift, F8 (Format). `SHIFT` + `F8`

• *Alt, =; Layout; Page.*

3. Press 2 (Page). `2`

4. Press 4 (Footer). `4`

   Press 1 (Footer A). `1`

5. Press 2 (Every Page). `2`

6. A blank screen appears.

7. Press Shift, F6 (Center). `SHIFT` + `F6`

8. Press Ctrl B. `CTRL` + `B`

9. Press F7 (Exit) twice. `F7` , `F7`

SUPPRESSED PAGE NUMBERING

1. Press Shift, F8 (Format). `SHIFT` + `F8`

• *Alt, =; Layout; Page.*

2. Press 2 (Page). `2`

3. Press 9 (Suppress).   `9`

    Press 8 (Suppress).   `8`

4. Press 1 (Suppress All Page Numbers).   `1`

5. Press Enter.   `ENTER`

6. Press F7 (Exit).   `F7`

7. Press Alt, F3, or F11   `ALT` + `F3`

    (Reveal Codes).   *or*   `F11`

PAGINATION ━━━━━━━━━━

NOTE: Pagination is automatic, with 54 lines on a page. If text is changed in any way, WordPerfect will readjust the text to 54 lines on each page.

1. If you do not want page to   `CTRL` + `ENTER`
    end where the program does,
    then insert page break (Hard
    Page) by pressing Ctrl, Enter.

PITCH/FONT ━━━━━━━━━━

1. Press Shift, F8 (Format).   `SHIFT` + `F8`

•   *Alt, =; Layout; Document.*

2. Press 3 (Document).   `3`

3. Press 3 (Initial Fonts).   ③

4. Make selection.   INPUT

5. Press Enter.   `ENTER`

6. Press F7 (Exit).   `F7`

PRINT
(Document on Screen)

1. Press Shift, F7 (Print Menu).   `SHIFT` + `F7`

- *Alt, =; File; Print.*

2. Press 1 (Full Text).   ①

PRINT — CANCEL
1. Press Shift, F7 (Print).   `SHIFT` + `F7`

- *Alt, =; File; Print.*

2. Press 4 (Control Printer).   ④

3. Press 1 (Cancel).   ①

4. Press Enter to cancel current printing.   `ENTER`

5. To cancel all print jobs, type an   `*` ,

   asterisk (*), then press Enter.   `ENTER`

PRINTER CONTROL MENU

1. Press Shift, F7 (Print).   SHIFT + F7
    *   *Alt, =; File; Print.*
2. Press 4 (Printer Control).   4
3. The following selections will appear at the bottom of the screen: Cancel Job(s), Rush Job, Display Jobs, Go (Start Printing), and Stop.

PRINTER - SELECT

1. Press Shift, F7 (Print).   SHIFT + F7
    *   *Alt, =; File; Print.*
2. Press S (Select Printer).   S
3. Highlight printer name.
4. Press 1 (Select).   1

PULL-DOWN MENU
(5.1 only)

1. Press Alt, Equals (=).   ALT + =
2. Make selection by highlighting word, then pressing Enter, or by typing the first letter of the word.

REDLINE ━━━━━━━━━━━━━━━━━━━━

NOTE: Redline is used to mark areas of text that must be approved after the printout.

WITH NEW TEXT
1. Press Shift, F8 (Format).   `SHIFT` + `F8`

- *Alt, =; Mark; Generate.*

2. Press 3 (Document).   `3`

3. Press 4 (Redline Method).   `4`

4. Select one of the 3 options.

5. Press F7 (Exit).   `F7`

AFTER TEXT HAS BEEN TYPED
1. Press Alt, F4, or F12 (Block).   `ALT` + `F4`
                                            or `F12`

2. Highlight text.

3. Press Ctrl, F8 (Font).   `CTRL` + `F8`

4. Press 2 (Appearance).   `2`

5. Press 8 (Redline).   `8`

REPLACE ━━━━━━━━━━━━━━━━━━━━

1. Place the cursor at the top of the document, position 1, line 1.

- *Alt, =; Search; Replace.*

2. Press Alt, F2 (Replace).   `ALT` + `F2`
3. Press Y to check each Replace, or   `Y`
   N to not check each Replace.   *or* `N`
4. Type word(s) you want to replace.   INPUT
5. Press F2 (Replace).   `F2`
6. Type replacement word(s).   INPUT
7. Press F2 (Replace).   `F2`
8. If a Y was pressed in step 3 to confirm   `Y`
   each case, then press Y to replace word   *or* `N`
   or press N not to replace word.

RETRIEVING A DOCUMENT

1. Press Shift, F10.   `SHIFT` + `F10`
- *Alt, =; File; Retrieve.*
2. Prompt reads "Document to be retrieved:".
3. Type document name.   INPUT
4. Press Enter.   `ENTER`

REVEAL CODES ═══════════

1. Press Alt, F3, or F11.   ⎡ ALT ⎤ + ⎡ F3 ⎤

                                                    or ⎡ F11 ⎤

* *Alt, =; Edit; Reveal Codes.*

2. Press Alt, F3, or F11 to turn   ⎡ ALT ⎤ + ⎡ F3 ⎤
    reveal codes off.   *or* ⎡ F11 ⎤

SAVE/CLEAR
SCREEN ═══════════════

1. Press F7 (Exit).   ⎡ F7 ⎤

* *Alt, =; File; Save.*

2. Prompt reads "Save Document? (Y/N) Y."

3. Press Y.   ⎡ Y ⎤

4. Prompt reads "Document to be saved:".

5. Type the filename. You may use up to   INPUT
    8 characters, with no spaces.

6. Press Enter.   ⎡ ENTER ⎤

7. Prompt reads "Exit WP? (Y/N) N."

8. Press N.   ⎡ N ⎤

9. Document is saved and screen is cleared.

SAVE/RETAIN DOCUMENT ON SCREEN ━━━━━━

1. Press F10.   `F10`

*   *Alt, =; File; Save.*

2. Prompt reads "Document to be saved:"

3. Type filename.   INPUT

4. Press Enter.   `ENTER`

SEARCH ━━━━━━━━━━━

1. For a forward search, place cursor under first char-
    acter at the beginning of the document. For a back-
    ward search, the cursor can be anywhere in the
    document.

*   *Alt, =; Search; Forwards; Backwards.*

2. Press F2 (Forward Search) or   `F2` *or*

    Shift, F2 (Backwards Search).   `SHIFT` + `F2`

3. Type the word(s) to search for.   INPUT

4. Press F2 (Forward Search) or   `F2` *or*

    Shift, F2 (Backwards Search).   `SHIFT` + `F2`

SETUP ════════════════════════

1. Press Shift, F1 (Setup).   `SHIFT` + `F1`

• *Alt, =; File; Setup.*

2. Press 5 (Initial Settings).   `5`

    Press 4 (Initial Settings).   `4`

    *NOTE: There are eight settings for WordPerfect 5.0
    and six for WordPerfect 5.1:*

    WordPerfect 5.0   *WordPerfect 5.1*
    1. Backup   1. Mouse
    2. Cursor speed   2. Display
    3. Display   3. Environment
    4. Fast save   4. Initial settings
    5. Initial settings   5. Keyboard layout
    6. Keyboard layout   6. Location of files
    7. Location of auxiliary files
    8. Units of measure

SHELL ════════════════════════

    *NOTE: The Shell key allows you to return
    to DOS without leaving WordPerfect.*

1. Press Ctrl, F1.   `CTRL` + `F1`

• *Alt, =; File; GoTo Dos.*

2. Press 1 (Go to DOS).   `1`

3. To get back to WordPerfect, type the   INPUT
    word EXIT.

SORT

NOTE: This entry contains four sub-entries for the following types of sorts: Ascending, descending; By line; By paragraph; By word. Refer to the sub-entry Sort-by-line for the most detailed sorting instructions. After Sort, the next main entry describes Sorts for Secondary merge files.

SORT — ASCENDING, DESCENDING
NOTE: Refer to Sort-by-line for more detailed sorting instructions.

1.	Press Ctrl, F9 (Sort).	`CTRL` + `F9`
•	*Alt, =; Tools; Sort.*	
2.	Press 2 (Sort).	`2`
3.	Press Enter (Scr as Input File).	`ENTER`
4.	Press Enter (Scr as Output File).	`ENTER`
5.	Press 3 (Keys).	`3`
6.	Enter information in all Key Fields.	INPUT
7.	Press F7 (Exit).	`F7`
8.	Press 6 (Order).	`6`
9.	Press 1 for Ascending or	`1`
	2 for Descending.	*or* `2`
10.	Press 1 (Perform Action).	`1`

SORT-BY-LINE

Line Sort when each record is on one line

1. Press Ctrl, F9 (Sort).   (CTRL) + (F9)

- *Alt, =; Tools; Sort.*

2. Press 2 (Sort).   (2)

3. Message reads "Input file to sort: (screen)".

    NOTE: Input file is the file to be sorted.
    It can be on the screen or on a disk.

4. Type input file, then   INPUT , (ENTER)
    press Enter.

5. Type output file, then   INPUT , (ENTER)
    press Enter.

    NOTE: The output file is the file that the
    sorted text will go to. It can be on the
    screen or on a disk.

6. Sort by line menu appears. There are 3
    columns: Key 1, Key 2, and Key 3. Each
    column has a Key, Typ, Field, and Word
    heading.

7. In the Key 1 column, Typ is "a" for   (A)

    Alphanumeric or "n" for numeric.   *or* (N)

    Field is "1", and Word is "1".

8. Press 7 (Type) if it is necessary to   (7)
    change type.

9. Press 3 (Keys) if necessary to change   (3)
    values.

10. Press 1 (Perform Action).   (1)

Example: Jones   Bossi
              Smith   Jones
              Bossi   Smith

Line Sort using second field

1. Press Ctrl, F9 (Sort).   (CTRL) + (F9)

• *Alt, =; Tools; Sort.*

2. Press 2 (Sort).   (2)

3. Press Enter. (Scr as Input File).   (ENTER)

4. Press Enter. (Scr as Output File).   (ENTER)

5. Press 3 (Keys).   (3)

6. Press Right Arrow once.   (→)

7. Type 2 under Field.   (2)

8. Press Right arrow once.   (→)

9. Type minus (-) 1.   (-), (1)

10. Key 1 will have Typ as "a" for alpha-
    numeric or "n" for numeric.

    Field is "2" and Word is "-1".

11. Press F7 (Exit).   (F7)

12. Press 1 (Perform Action).   (1)

Example: Tom Jones   Ed Adams
              Amy Smith   Tom Jones
              Ed Adams   Amy Smith

SORT-BY-PARAGRAPH
NOTE: Refer to Sort-by-line for more detailed sorting instructions.

1. Place cursor under first character in paragraph.

2. Press Ctrl, F9 (Sort).   `CTRL` + `F9`

3. Press 2 (Sort).   `2`

4. Press Enter (Scr as Input File).   `ENTER`

5. Press Enter (Scr as Output File).   `ENTER`

6. Press 7 (Type).   `7`

7. Press 3 (Paragraph).   `3`

8. Sort by paragraph menu appears.

9. Press 3 (Keys).   `3`

10. Press Right Arrow, then type 1   `→` , `1`
for Line.

11. Press Right Arrow, then type 2   `→` , `2`
for Field.

12. Press Right Arrow, then type   `→` , `-` , `1`
minus (-) one.

13. Press Right Arrow to get to Key 2.   `→`

14. Press Right Arrow, and "a" appears   `→`
under Type.

15. Press Right Arrow, and 1 appears in   `→`
Line, Field and Word columns.

16. Press F7 (Exit).   `F7`

17. Press 6 (Order).   `6`

18. Press 1 for Ascending or   ①

    2 for (Descending).   *or* ②

19. Press 1 (Perform Action).   ①

SORT-BY-WORD

NOTE: Sort by word when last name isn't always the second word, as in "Robert D. Gill". Refer to Sort-by-line for more detailed sorting instructions.

1.   Press Ctrl, F9 (Sort).   (CTRL) + (F9)

 • *Alt, =; Tools; Sort.*

2.   Press 2 (Sort).   ②

3.   Press Enter (Scr as Input File).   (ENTER)

4.   Press Enter (Scr as Output File).   (ENTER)

5.   Press 3 (Keys).   ③

6.   Press Right Arrow, then type 1, 2 or 3   (→)

    depending on where word in the Field   ① ,

    column is positioned.   ② *or* ③

7.   Press Right Arrow, then type minus (-)   (→) ,

    one in Word column to indicate first   (-) , ①
    word to right.

8.   Press Right Arrow once, Field is 1,   (→)

    Word is 1, 2, *or* 3 depending on   ① ,

    word position.   ② *or* ③

9.   Press F7 (Exit).   (F7)

10. Type 1 (Perform Action).   ①

SORT — SECONDARY MERGE FILE

NOTE: This converts a database file to a secondary merge file to be sorted or to be used with a primary merge file to produce a new file.

STEP ONE: Convert Database File

1. Retrieve the database file, and place cursor under the first character in the file.

2. Press Alt, F2 (Replace). `ALT` + `F2`

3. Press N (Not to Confirm). `N`

4. Prompt reads: "Srch:".

5. Press Enter (Search String). `ENTER`

6. Press Esc. `ESC`

7. Prompt reads: "Replace with:".

8. Press Ctrl, E, then press `CTRL` + `E`

   Enter. `ENTER`

10. Press Esc. `ESC`

11. Press Home, Home, Up Arrow `HOME` ,

    to getback to the beginning of `HOME` ,

    the document. `↑`

12. Press Alt, F2 (Replace). `ALT` + `F2`

13. Press N. `N`

14. Press Tab. `TAB`

15. Press Esc.   (ESC)

16. Press F9 (^R), then Enter.   (F9) , (ENTER)

17. Press Esc.   (ESC)

18. The secondary Merge File is now ready
    to be sorted.

STEP TWO: Sort Merge

1. Press Ctrl, F9 (Sort).   (CTRL) + (F9)

- *Alt, =; Tools; Sort.*

2. Press 2 (Sort).   (2)

3. Press Enter (Scr as Input File).   (ENTER)

4. Press Enter (Scr as Output File).   (ENTER)

5. Press 7 (Type).   (7)

6. Press 1 (Merge).   (1)

7. Press 3 (Keys).   (3)

8. Enter information in Key Fields.   INPUT

9. Key 1 will show as "a,1,1,1" (Sort by Last
   Name). Key 2 will show as "a,2,1,1":

10. Press F7 (Exit).   (F7)

11. Press 1 (Perform Action).   (1)

SPELL CHECK ━━━━━━━━━

1. Document to be checked should be on
   the screen.

- *Alt, =; Tools; Spell.*

2. Press Ctrl, F2 (Spell).   `CTRL` + `F2`

3. Press 3 (Document).   `3`

4. Message reads "Please Wait".

5. When Speller does not recognize a
    word, the word will be highlighted.

    Press 1 to skip the word once.   `1`

    Press 2 to skip all occurrences of word. `2`

    Press 3 to add the word to the Speller.   `3`

    Press 4 to access editing screen where   `4` ,
       normal editing can take place. Press
       F7 when you want to return to the Speller. `F7`

    Press 5 to lookup. Type the first letters   `5` ,
       of a word, followed by an asterisk
       (e.g., hap* to get a list of words that   INPUT
       begin with hap).

6. When the spelling check has been completed, the
    message "Word count: 00." appears. Press any key
    to continue appears at the bottom of the screen.

SPLIT SCREEN ════════
(Windows)

1. Have cursor in Document 1.

- *Alt, =; Layout.*

2. Press Ctrl, F3 (Screen).   ⌐CTRL¬ + ⌐F3¬

3. Press 1 (Window).   ⌐1¬

4. Type number of lines you want in   INPUT
    window (usually 11).

5. Press Enter.   ⌐ENTER¬

6. Press Shift, F3 (Switch) to move   ⌐SHIFT¬ + ⌐F3¬
    between documents.

7. When you want to return to the   ⌐CTRL¬ + ⌐F3¬
    full screen, press Ctrl, F3
    (Screen).

8. Press 1 (Window).   ⌐1¬

9. Type 24 for number of lines.   INPUT

SPREADSHEET —
IMPORT/LINK
(5.1 only)

NOTE: WordPerfect 5.1 can import/link the following spreadsheet programs:

•Lotus 1,2,3 (V1.0, 2.2)
•Microsoft Excel (V2.X)
•PlanPerfect

A spreadsheet file can be IMPORTED only once.
A spreadsheet LINKED filed can be updated and
transported.

1. Place cursor where spreadsheet is to appear.
2. Press Ctrl, F5 (Text In/Out). `CTRL` + `F5`
3. Press 5 (Spreadsheet). `5`
4. Press 1 for Import or 2 for Link. `1` *or* `2`
5. Press 1 (Filename). `1`
6. Type spreadsheet filename (e.g. a:\<filename>). INPUT
7. Press 2 (Range). `2`
8. Type spreadsheet range to import/link. INPUT
9. Press 3 (Type). `3`
10. Press 1 for Table or 2 for Text. `1` *or* `2`
11. Press 4 (Perform Import or Link). `4`

STRIKEOUT

1. Place cursor under first character to be struck out.
2. Press Alt, F4, or F12 (Block). `ALT` + `F4`
   or `F12`
3. Highlight text.
4. Press Ctrl, F8 (Font). `CTRL` + `F8`
5. Press 2 (Appearance). `2`
6. Press 9 (Strikeout). `9`

SUBSCRIPT ━━━━━━━━

1. Before typing the character to be subscripted, press Ctrl, F8 (Font).   `CTRL` + `F8`

- *Alt, =; Font; Subscript.*

2. Press 1 (Size).   `1`
3. Press 2 (Subscript).   `2`
4. Type the character.   INPUT
5. Press Ctrl, F8 (Font).   `CTRL` + `F8`
6. Press 3 (Normal).   `3`

SUPERSCRIPT ━━━━━━━━

1. Before typing the character to be superscripted, press Ctrl, F8 (Font).   `CTRL` + `F8`

- *Alt, =; Font; Superscript.*

2. Press 1 (Size).   `1`
3. Press 1 (Superscript).   `1`
4. Type the character.   INPUT
5. Press Ctrl, F8 (Font).   `CTRL` + `F8`
6. Press 3 (Normal).   `3`

SUPPRESS
For Current Page Only

NOTE: Use when you do not want a header, footer, or page number on a page.

1. Press Shift, F8 (Format). $\boxed{\text{SHIFT}}$ + $\boxed{\text{F8}}$

- *Alt, =; Layout; Page.*

2. Press 2 (Page). $\boxed{2}$

3. Press 9 (Suppress). $\boxed{9}$

   Press 8 (Suppress). $\boxed{8}$

4. Press 1. $\boxed{1}$

5. Press F7 (Exit) twice to return $\boxed{\text{F7}}$, $\boxed{\text{F7}}$
   to document.

   Press F7 once. $\boxed{\text{F7}}$

SWITCH
DOCUMENTS

1. Press Shift, F3 (Switch). $\boxed{\text{SHIFT}}$ + $\boxed{\text{F3}}$

2. "Doc 2 Page 1" appears. Any text
   on this page does not print.

TABS

CENTER TAB

*NOTE: This centers column headings
for all columns across the page.*

1. Press Shift, F8 (Format). `SHIFT` + `F8`

- *Alt, =; Layout; Line.*

2. Press 1 (Line). `1`

3. Press 8 (Tabs). `8`

4. Press Ctrl, End (Clear All Tabs). `CTRL` + `END`

5. Type position for tab. INPUT

6. Press Tab. `TAB`

7. Type "C" over the "L". `C`

8. Press F7 twice (Exit). `F7` , `F7`

DECIMAL TAB

1. Press Shift, F8 (Format). `SHIFT` + `F8`

- *Alt, =; Layout; Line.*

2. Press 1 (Line). `1`

3. Press 8 (Tabs). `8`

4. Press Ctrl, End (Clear Tabs). `CTRL` + `END`

5. Type position for tab. INPUT

6. Press Tab `TAB`

7. Type a "D" at position for decimal tab. `D`

8. Press F7 (Exit) twice. `F7` , `F7`

DOT LEADER TAB

1. Press Shift, F8 (Format).   `SHIFT` + `F8`

*   *Alt, =; Layout; Line.*

2. Press 1 (Line).   `1`

3. Press 8 (Tabs).   `8`

4. Press Ctrl, End (Clear all tabs).   `CTRL` + `END`

5. Type the number position you   INPUT ,

    want the tab at, then press Tab.   `TAB`

6. Type an "R" over the "L".   `R`

7. Press a Period. The R is highlighted,   `.`
    and right tab has been entered
    preceded by a dot leader.

TABLE COLUMNS ━━━━━━

STEP ONE: Formatting Table Columns
(Calculating Tab Settings for Columns)

1. Press Shift, F6 (Center).   `SHIFT` + `F6`

2. Type the longest line in each column   INPUT
    and the number of spaces between
    each column.

3. Move the cursor to the first character of
    each column and note the position num-
    ber for each column. For numbers with
    decimals, move cursor to decimal posi-
    tion.

4. Delete the table-format line and   `DELETE`
   center instruction.

5. Press Alt, F3, or F11 to verify   `ALT` + `F3`
   format line and center delete.   *or* `F11`

6. Press Shift, F8 (Format).   `SHIFT` + `F8`

7. Press 1 (Line).   `1`

8. Press 8 (Tabs).   `8`

9. Clear all tabs by pressing   `CTRL` + `END`
   Ctrl, End.

10. Set tabs (L for text and D for   `L` *or* `D`
    decimal tabs).

11. Press F7 twice.   `F7` , `F7`

12. Press Alt, F3, or F11 to verify tab   `ALT` + `F3`
    settings (Reveal Codes).   *or* `F11`

STEP TWO: Typing Text For Table

13. Type text for table. If calculations need
    to be made, follow steps 14 to 23.

14. Press Alt, F7 (Math/Columns).   `ALT` + `F7`

15. Press 2 (Math Def).   `2`

    Press 3 (Math).   `3`

    Press 3 (Define).   `3`

16. Math definition menu appears. Each col-
    umn is marked by a letter a through x.
    Column type is defaulted as 2 for numeric;
    Type 1 if the text is to be alphanumeric.

17. Press F7 (Exit).   F7
18. Press 1 (Math On).   1
19. Press Alt, F3, or F11 to verify   ALT + F3
    Math On (Reveal Codes).   *or* F11
20. Press Alt, F3 to exit Reveal Codes. ALT + F3
21. Type the table, pressing Tab   INPUT ,
    before each column.   TAB
22. Press Alt, F7 (Math/Columns).   ALT + F7
23. Press 1 (Math Off).   1
    Press 3 (Math).   3
    Press 2 (Columns).   2

TABLES ═══════════
(5.1 only)

NOTE: The table consists of horizontal rows and vertical columns. These rows and columns create cells.

CREATE TABLE
1. Place cursor at the left margin where you want the table.

2. Press Alt, F7 (Columns/Tabs).   `ALT` + `F7`
3. Press 2 (Tables).   `2`
4. Press 1 (Create).   `1`
5. Type number of columns, then   INPUT ,
    press Enter.   `ENTER`
6. Type number of rows, then   INPUT ,
    press Enter.   `ENTER`
    Press F7 (Exit).   `F7`

EDIT TABLE
1. Place cursor in the table.
2. Press Alt, F7 (Columns/Table).   `ALT` + `F7`
•   *Alt, =; Layout; Tables; Edit.*
3. Choose function from the menu at   INPUT
    the bottom of the screen.

FORMAT COLUMNS AND CELLS
1. Place cursor in the table.
2. Press Alt, F7 (Columns/Table).   `ALT` + `F7`
3. Press Alt, F4, or F12 (Block).   `ALT` + `F4`
    or `F12`
4. Highlight cells or columns.
5. Press 2 (Format).   `2`
6. Press 1 for Cell or 2 for Columns.   `1` *or* `2`
7. Choose a function and type text.   INPUT

MATH CALCULATIONS IN TABLE

1. Place cursor in the cell where the calculation is to take place.

2. Press Alt, F7 (Columns/Table). $\boxed{\text{ALT}}$ + $\boxed{\text{F7}}$

3. Press 5 (Math). $\boxed{5}$

4. Choose function from menu at the bottom of the screen.

   Press 1 to calculate (recalculates original formula). $\boxed{1}$

   Press 2 to enter formula (e.g., A1 + A2...B4, B7). $\boxed{2}$

   Press 3 to copy formula. $\boxed{3}$

   Press 4. Plus (+) adds column. Word-Perfect treats this as a subtotal. $\boxed{4}$

   Press 5. Equals (=) gives total of subtotals. $\boxed{5}$

   Press 6. Asterisk (*) multiplies. $\boxed{6}$

TABLE OF AUTHORITIES (ToA)

NOTE: Table of Authority is used in legal briefs to mark where citations and statutes are located in the brief. There are four steps to prepare a Table of Authority (ToA).

STEP ONE: Setup for ToA
1. Press Shift, F1 (Setup).   `SHIFT` + `F1`

2. Press 5 (Initial Settings).   `5`

   Press 4 (Initial Settings).   `4`

3. Press 6 (ToA).   `6`

   Press 7 (ToA).   `7`

4. Select 1 for Dot Leaders, 2 for Under-   `1` ,
   lining, or 3 for Blank Line between   `2` *or* `3`
   Authorities.

5. Press Enter.   `ENTER`

6. Press F7 (Exit).   `F7`

STEP TWO: Mark Text
NOTE: Most ToA markings should be done after document is finished. Two methods are shown below.

Method One
1. Place cursor under the first character to be marked.

2. Press Alt, F4, or F12 (Block). $\boxed{\text{ALT}}$ + $\boxed{\text{F4}}$

    or $\boxed{\text{F12}}$

3. Highlight text, then press Alt, F5 $\boxed{\text{ALT}}$ + $\boxed{\text{F5}}$
    (Mark Text).

4. Press 4 (ToA). $\boxed{4}$

* *Alt, =; Mark; ToA; Mark Full.*

5. Press Enter to accept the short form. $\boxed{\text{ENTER}}$

6. Type in the short form.   INPUT

7. Press Enter. $\boxed{\text{ENTER}}$

8. Repeat steps 1 to 7.

Method Two: Extended Search
1. After document is finished, place cursor
    at the top of the document.

2. Press Home, F2 (Extended $\boxed{\text{HOME}}$ + $\boxed{\text{F2}}$
    Search)

3. Type search words.   INPUT

4. Press F2 (Search). $\boxed{\text{F2}}$

5. Press Alt, F5 (Block). $\boxed{\text{ALT}}$ + $\boxed{\text{F5}}$

6. Press 4 (Short Form). $\boxed{4}$

* *Alt, =; Mark; ToA; Mark Short.*

7. Press Enter. $\boxed{\text{ENTER}}$

8. Repeat steps 1 to 7.

    *NOTE: Keep a list of the marked cases
    to avoid duplicates.*

STEP THREE: Define ToA

1. At the bottom of the page before the ToA, press Ctrl, Enter (Page Break). ⎡CTRL⎤ + ⎡ENTER⎤

2. Press Shift, F6 (Center). ⎡SHIFT⎤ + ⎡F6⎤

3. Type the title. INPUT

4. Mark the title following the Mark Text directions above.

5. Press Enter three times. ⎡ENTER⎤ , ⎡ENTER⎤ , ⎡ENTER⎤

6. Type the first section heading, then press Enter. INPUT , ⎡ENTER⎤

7. Press Alt, F5 (Mark Text). ⎡ALT⎤ + ⎡F5⎤

8. Press 5 (Define). ⎡5⎤

9. Press 4 (Define ToA). ⎡4⎤

10. Press Enter. ⎡ENTER⎤

11. The definition for table of authorities 1 appears. (1-16)

12. Press Enter. ⎡ENTER⎤

13. Repeat steps 6 to 12 for each section.

STEP FOUR: Generate ToA

1. Save document.

2. Press Alt, F5 (Mark Text). ⎡ALT⎤ + ⎡F5⎤

• *Alt, =; Mark; Generate.*

3. Press 6 (Generate). ⎡6⎤

4. Press 5 (Generate Tables, Indexes, Auto Ref). $\boxed{5}$

5. Message reads "Exiting tables, lists, and indexes will be replaced. Continue? Y/N". Type Y. $\boxed{Y}$

6. When generating is done, the document appears on the screen with all tables and lists.

7. Press F10 (Save). $\boxed{F10}$

TABLE OF CONTENTS ════════

NOTE: Three functions must be performed to get a Table of Contents: Mark, Define, and Generate.

STEP ONE: Mark Text

1. Place the cursor under the first character of the text to be listed in the table of contents.

2. Press Alt, F4, or F12 (Block). $\boxed{ALT} + \boxed{F4}$
    or $\boxed{F12}$

3. Highlight text.

4. Press Alt, F5 (Mark Text). $\boxed{ALT} + \boxed{F5}$

5. Press 1 for ToC (Table of Contents). $\boxed{1}$

• *Alt, =; Mark; ToC.*

6. Prompt reads "toc Level:"

7. Press 1 for Level 1, then Enter.   (1) , (ENTER)

8. Repeat steps 1 to 7 for all text to be
    in the table of contents.

STEP TWO: Define Numbering Style

1. Place the cursor in the document where
    the table of contents is to appear.

2. Press Ctrl, Enter to create a   (CTRL) + (ENTER)
    new page for table of contents.

3. Press Shift, F8 (Format).   (SHIFT) + (F8)

4. Press 2 (Page).   (2)

5. Press 6 (New Page Number).   (6)

    Press 1 (New Page Number).   (1)

6. Type "i" for lower case Roman   (i)
    numbers.

7. Press Shift, F6 (Center).   (SHIFT) + (F6)

8. Type "Table of Contents". Press   INPUT ,
    Enter three times.   (ENTER) ,
    (ENTER) , (ENTER)

9. Press Alt, F5 (Mark Text).   (ALT) + (F5)

•   *Alt, =; Mark; ToC.*

10. Press 5 (Define).   (5)

11. Press 1 (ToC).   ☐ 1

Omit Step 11.

12. Press 1 (Number of Levels).   ☐ 1

13. Press 5.   ☐ 5

14. Press Ctrl, Enter to end ToC.   [CTRL] + [ENTER]

STEP THREE: Generate Table of Contents

1. Place the cursor at the location in the document where the table of contents is to appear.

2. Press Alt, F5 (Mark text).   [ALT] + [F5]

• *Alt, =; Mark; Generate.*

3. Press 6 (Generate).   ☐ 6

4. Press 5 (Generate Tables, Indexes, Automatic References).   ☐ 5

5. Prompt reads "Existing tables lists and indexes will be replaced. Continue (Y/N) Y".

6. Type a Y.   ☐ Y

7. Message reads "Generation in progress." The Counter appears.

8. The table of contents appears where the cursor was located in the document.

9. Press F10 (Save).   [F10]

TEXT IN/OUT ———

NOTE: Text in/out (Ctrl, F5) converts Lotus 1-2-3, dBase, and other word processing software into:
- *DOS text files*
- *Wordperfect's text in/out files*
- *Wordperfect's convert facilities in other software.*

STEP ONE: Lotus 1-2-3 Conversion
NOTE: You may lose underline, bold, and other formating in the transfer of text.

1. You must be in Lotus 1-2-3 and have the spreadsheet on the screen. The 1-2-3 file must be converted to a print file first.

2. Press / (Menu). $\boxed{/}$

3. Press P (Print). $\boxed{P}$

4. Press F (File). $\boxed{F}$

5. Type the name of the file to be converted to a print file. Make sure you use the full path name (e.g. a:\sales.wk1).

6. Press Enter. $\boxed{ENTER}$

7. Press R (Range), then type the range $\boxed{R}$,
   of the spreadsheet to be converted.   INPUT

8. Press O (Options). $\boxed{O}$

9. Press O (Other). $\boxed{O}$

10. Press U (Unformatted). $\boxed{U}$

11. Press M (Margins). Change left $\boxed{M}$, INPUT ,
    margin to zero, then press Enter. $\boxed{ENTER}$

12. Press M (Margins). Change right margin (The right margin can not be more than 240), then press Enter. $\boxed{M}$, INPUT , $\boxed{ENTER}$

13. Press Q (Quit). $\boxed{Q}$

14. Press G (Go). $\boxed{G}$

15. Press Q (Quit). This brings you back to the spreadsheet screen. $\boxed{Q}$

16. Press / (Menu). $\boxed{/}$

17. Press Q (Quit). $\boxed{Q}$

18. Press Y (Yes). $\boxed{Y}$

NOTE: A print file has a PRN extension name.

STEP TWO: Retrieve Spreadsheet File

Method One
1. Open the WordPerfect program. Retrieve the file you want the spreadsheet in.

2. Place the cursor where the spreadsheet is to appear.

3. Press F5 (List Files). $\boxed{F5}$

4. Highlight the PRN file.

5. Press 5 (Text/In). $\boxed{F5}$

Method Two
1. Press Ctrl, F5 (Text/In). $\boxed{CTRL}$ + $\boxed{F5}$

2. Press 1 (DOS). $\boxed{1}$

3. Press 2 (Retrieve). $\boxed{2}$

DBASE CONVERSION

1. Get into the dBase program. At the   INPUT
   dot (.) prompt, type USE <filename>.

2. Type REPORT FORM <filename> TO   INPUT
   FILE <new filename>.

3. Follow steps 1 to 5 under Step Two above.

CREATING & RETRIEVING DOS TEXT FILES

1. Press Ctrl, F5 (Text/in).   `CTRL` + `F5`

2. Press 1 (Dos text).   `1`

3. Press 1 (Save).   `1`

THESAURUS ═══════════

1. Place cursor anywhere in the word to
   be checked.

2. Press Alt, F1 (Thesaurus).   `ALT` + `F1`

- *Alt, =; Tools; Thesaurus*

3. A column of words appear.

4. Press 1 (Replace).   `1`

5. Prompt reads "Press letter for word."

6. Press the letter that corresponds to   INPUT
   the replacement word.

TOP MARGIN

1. Press Shift, F8 (Format).   `SHIFT` + `F8`
*   *Alt, =; Layout.*
2. Press 2 (Page).   `2`
3. Press 5 (Top Margin).   `5`
4. Type number.   INPUT
5. Press Enter twice.   `ENTER` , `ENTER`
6. Press F7 (Exit).   `F7`

TYPEOVER

1. Press Ins.   `INS`
2. Type new text over old text to make   INPUT
    correction.
3. Press Ins to get back to the insert mode.   `INS`

UNDELETE

1. Place cursor where you want deleted
    text to be recalled.
2. Press F1 (Cancel).   `F1`

3.   Press 1 to Restore Deleted Text or   `1`

     2 to Delete Previous Text.   *or* `2`

UNDERLINE ━━━━━━━━━━

BEFORE TYPING TEXT
1.   Press F8.   `F8`

2.   Type text.   INPUT

3.   Press F8.   `F8`

AFTER TYPING TEXT
1.   Place cursor under first character to
     be underlined.

2.   Press Alt, F4, or F12 (Block).   `ALT` + `F4`

                                               or `F12`

3.   Highlight text to be underlined.

4.   Press F8.   `F8`

UNDERLINE—DELETE
1.   Press Alt, F3, or F11 (Reveal   `ALT` + `F3`

     Codes).   *or* `F11`

2.   Place cursor on underline codes (Und).

3.   Press Delete.   `DELETE`

4.   Press F1 (Cancel) if you want to   `F1`
     restore deletion.

VIEW DOCUMENT ═══

1. Place cursor in the document.
2. Press Shift, F7 (Print).   `SHIFT` + `F7`
*   *Alt, =; File; Print.*
3. Press 6 (View).   `6`

WIDOWS AND ORPHANS ═══

1. Move cursor to the top of document.
*   *Alt, =; Layout; Line.*
2. Press Shift, F8 (Format).   `SHIFT` + `F8`
3. Press 1 (Line).   `1`
4. Press 9 (Widow/Orphan Protection).   `9`
5. Type Y for Yes to turn off widows   `Y`
    and orphans.
6. Press F7 (Exit).   `F7`

INDEX